LITERATURE AND THE REMAINS OF THE DEATH PENALTY

D0743390

 INVENTING WRITING THEORY

Jacques Lezra and Paul North, series editors

LITERATURE AND THE REMAINS OF THE DEATH PENALTY

PEGGY KAMUF

Fordham University Press   *New York 2019*

Copyright © 2019 Fordham University Press

All rights reserved. No part of this publication may be reproduced, stored in a retrieval system, or transmitted in any form or by any means—electronic, mechanical, photocopy, recording, or any other—except for brief quotations in printed reviews, without the prior permission of the publisher.

Fordham University Press has no responsibility for the persistence or accuracy of URLs for external or third-party Internet websites referred to in this publication and does not guarantee that any content on such websites is, or will remain, accurate or appropriate.

Fordham University Press also publishes its books in a variety of electronic formats. Some content that appears in print may not be available in electronic books.

Visit us online at www.fordhampress.com.

Library of Congress Cataloging-in-Publication Data

Names: Kamuf, Peggy, 1947– author.
Title: Literature and the remains of the death penalty / Peggy Kamuf.
Description: First edition. | New York : Fordham University Press, 2019. | Series: Idiom: inventing writing theory | Includes bibliographical references and index.
Identifiers: LCCN 2018010819| ISBN 9780823282302 (cloth : alk. paper) | ISBN 9780823282296 (pbk. : alk. paper)
Subjects: LCSH: Capital punishment in literature. | American fiction—20th century—History and criticism.
Classification: LCC PS374.C357 K36 2019 | DDC 809/.933556—dc23
LC record available at https://lccn.loc.gov/2018010819

Printed in the United States of America

21 20 19   5 4 3 2 1

First edition

CONTENTS

Every language artist is an artist of the struggle against the condemnation to death.

—Hélène Cixous

INTRODUCTION

Like many if not all books, this one began in another book, Jacques Derrida's *Death Penalty, Volume I*, which is the transcript of the first year of a seminar given from 1999–2000.[1] I have had a long and varied relationship with this book over the past almost twenty years. I first heard these lectures at UC Irvine, in two successive spring quarters when Derrida was in residence there and reprised in English the lectures he had written and delivered initially in French, at the École des Hautes Études en Sciences Sociales in Paris. As auditors, already, the lectures made a strong impression on the mostly American audience in California, if I may judge by my own response. Because the issue of the death penalty had and still has urgent pertinence here, where it remains in actual practice under the law of many states and the federal government, Derrida repeatedly challenged his listeners to question this singular remainder of capital punishment in a world that has widely abolished it. When he delivered the lectures for his UC Irvine audience, this American context often pressed itself on the analysis, for the death penalty that year was frequently in the news. No one could have realized then, however, that 1999 would in fact set the mark for the most executions in the United States in any year since 1977, when *Gregg v.*

---

1. Jacques Derrida, *Séminaire, La peine de mort, Volume I (1999–2000)*, ed. Geoffrey Bennington, Marc Crépon, and Thomas Dutoit (Paris: Éditions Galilée, 2012).

Georgia effectively allowed them to resume.[2] This highpoint, so to speak, being reached in the execution chambers of the U.S. justice system regularly left its mark on the seminar.

Later, when I was able to read the typescripts of the lectures, this mark especially held my attention. It signaled a particular place, I ventured, in the actual struggle over the U.S. death penalty, a location that Derrida could not have named precisely in 1999 but that his analysis nevertheless points us to. I sought to work this out in an essay that brought Derrida's analysis of what he called the anesthesial logic of the modern death penalty into line with the crisis currently shutting off the supply of anesthetic for lethal injections in the United States.[3] That essay was a first attempt to respond in writing to the seminar, to let its reflections extend into the present, where the U.S. death penalty continues its agony. I made other such efforts, the most sustained being a translation of the first volume of the seminar, which was published in 2013 after three years of work.[4]

Once *The Death Penalty* existed as an English book, I designed a graduate seminar in comparative literature around it. I titled it "Literature and the Death Penalty,"[5] which was not just out of disciplinary compliance. As I outline in detail in Chapter 1, Derrida's seminar repeatedly takes its lead from literature and literary texts.[6]

2. See the website of the Death Penalty Information Center for a wealth of statistics about the death penalty in the United States: http://www.deathpenaltyinfo.org/documents/Fact Sheet.pdf.

3. See my "Protocol: Death Penalty Addiction," *Southern Journal of Philosophy* 50, Spindel Supplement (2012): 5–19; and "The Heart of the Death Penalty," *Oxford Literary Review*, ed. Peggy Kamuf, 35, no. 2 (2013).

4. Jacques Derrida, *The Death Penalty, Volume I*, ed. Geoffrey Bennington and Thomas Dutoit, trans. Peggy Kamuf (Chicago: University of Chicago Press, 2013); hereafter *DP I*. The translation benefited immeasurably from the collective efforts of the Derrida Seminars Translation Project at two summer workshops, in July 2010 and 2011.

5. This seminar, conducted at the University of Southern California in the spring of 2014, was offered in the Comparative Studies in Literature and Culture Doctoral Program as CSLC 602.

6. In the second year of his seminar, this preoccupation with literature has largely receded. Instead, Derrida devotes far more space than he had in the first volume to psychoanalytic texts by Freud but also Theodor Reik and Sándor Ferenczi. Derrida calls attention to this change of

Our own seminar followed Derrida's closely, especially for its readings of literary texts, but we also adopted the principle of supple-
menting his reading list with other works. I added the short text by
George Orwell "A Hanging," Kafka's "In the Penal Colony," Baudelaire's prose poem "A Heroic Death," and Hugo's *The Last Day of a
Condemned Man*, a text that Derrida leaves aside in his long discussions of this writer. The students in the seminar added other texts:
Roberto Bolaño's *The Part about the Crimes*, from *2666*; Oscar
Wilde's *Salome*; Krzysztof Kieślowski's *A Short Film about Killing*;
and many others. After the seminar ended, I kept thinking about the
topic and before long realized I had begun to imagine this book in
my head. Soon enough I started writing it, and its first two chapters
came quickly because they could be drawn straight from the seminar. But I did not see where it would turn in subsequent chapters,
in which I wanted to focus each time on a specific literary work.

Meanwhile, I was reading everything I came upon that might set
me on a fruitful path. I lingered long with *Invitation to a Beheading*, which was the first of his novels that Vladimir Nabokov translated into English. As a somewhat conscientious comparatist, however, I could not think about writing seriously on this fascinating
novel, which I was able to read only in translation, albeit a translation by the author.[7] I had to stay with what I could track closest to
ground level, in the grain of an idiom, for I believe that is where
literary language is most disruptive of expectations and thus most
productive for a new thinking against the death penalty, which is
what I was after. Literary historical studies like John Cyril Barton's

---

focus when, toward end of the second year, he recalls the "question that we posed last year,
namely, the following: how is it that the abolitionist cause has more often been served, publicly
served, by poets or by writers than by philosophers and even politicians?" *The Death Penalty,
Volume II*, ed. Geoffrey Bennington and Marc Crépon, trans. Elizabeth Rottenberg (Chicago:
University of Chicago Press, 2017), 232.

7. Nabokov was caustic about the failings of translation, including his own. His poem "On
Translating *Eugene Onegin*" begins: "What is translation? On a platter / A poet's pale and glar-
ing head, / A parrot's screech, a monkey's chatter, / And profanation of the dead." *New Yorker*,
January 8, 1955.

Literary Executions: Capital Punishment and American Culture, 1820–1925 and David Guest's *Sentenced to Death: The American Novel and Capital Punishment* helped me probe the American example.[8] Bolstered by legal histories like Stuart Banner's *The Death Penalty: An American Institution,*[9] these literary studies accumulated insight into the specifically American institution of capital punishment, which I was coming somewhat reluctantly to recognize as perhaps the most pertinent framing of the book I was trying to write. I say "reluctantly" because the pertinence of the questions I wanted to raise and worry with this book could not be contained, so I believed, by the peculiarity of the American context and the very particular history there of the persistence of a legal death penalty.

The reluctance to feature the American experience of the death penalty dissolved more or less when I read Robert Coover's extraordinary 1977 novel *The Public Burning* (see Chapter 3). This exhaustively researched fictional recasting opens on the eve of the day, June 18, 1953, originally set for the execution in the electric chair of Ethel and Julius Rosenberg at Sing Sing prison for the crime of espionage. Coover, however, has exercised the extreme fictional license of moving the execution from a prison enclosure into the open of Times Square and staging there a hyperbolic public spectacle, which one can read as the correlative of the frenzied atmosphere that surrounded the Rosenbergs' arrest, prosecution, conviction, sentencing, imprisonment, and final punishment. Although legal wrangling with the publisher delayed it, Coover's novel had first been scheduled to appear in 1976, the American bicentennial year, which also happens to be the year the Supreme Court issued the opinion in *Gregg v. Georgia* that in essence restarted executions

---

8. Cyril Barton, *Literary Executions: Capital Punishment and American Culture* (Baltimore, Md.: Johns Hopkins University Press, 2014); David Guest, *Sentenced to Death: The American Novel and Capital Punishment* (Oxford: University Press of Mississippi, 1997).

9. Stuart Banner, *The Death Penalty: An American Institution* (Cambridge, Mass.: Harvard University Press, 2003).

in the country after a ten-year de facto moratorium. Naturally, this coincidence is nowhere remarked in the novel itself, whose meticulous reconstruction of the Rosenberg "affair" stays strictly within its historical frame. Nevertheless, it weighed on the scale with which I had begun to measure the novel's pertinence for the post-*Gregg* era of the American death penalty, during which the secrecy surrounding executions has, over the past decade, reached a high degree of obsessiveness in state legislatures and among prison authorities. An important precipitating factor for all this secrecy, as I had analyzed in my earlier essay, was the withdrawal from the market of the anesthetic favored in lethal injection, the execution method invented in the wake of *Gregg*. With its central device of hyperpublicity, *The Public Burning* inverts this drive toward secrecy and, in the process, which is the process of fiction, exposes phantasmatic investments that maintain and sustain the practice of the death penalty. For if indeed, as Derrida argues, the death penalty survives on the strength of a phantasm, which is the phantasm of a sovereign power over death and the end of finitude,[10] then it draws on the power of fiction. It is a phantasm, however, insofar as it disavows the fiction in favor of belief. Fiction that does not disavow but rather remarks itself, fiction such as *The Public Burning*, can make readable the phantasm as such, as well as its remains.

If the coincidence between the publication of Coover's novel and the resumption of executions in the United States was just that, a coincidence, the same can most definitely not be said of Norman Mailer's enormous novel *The Executioner's Song*, published three years after the decision, in 1979 (see Chapter 4). On the contrary, the novel owes its very existence to *Gregg*: Its subject is the last

---

10. See *DP I*, 257–258; see also Gwynne Fulton, "'Phantasmatics': Sovereignty and the Image of Death in Derrida's Death Penalty Seminars," *Mosaic* 48, no. 3 (September 2015); and Michael Naas, "The Philosophy and Literature of the Death Penalty: Two Sides of the Same Sovereign," *Southern Journal of Philosophy*, Spindel Supplement, vol. 50 (2012); as well as "*Comme si, comme ça*: Following Derrida on the Phantasms of the Self, the State, and a Sovereign God," in Naas, *Derrida from Now On* (New York: Fordham University Press, 2008).

nine months of the life of the man, Gary Gilmore, who was the first to be executed under this new dispensation of American capital punishment.

The work of Coover and the work of Mailer occupy very different places in the landscape of contemporary American fiction: the former is usually pigeonholed—often so as to dismiss it—as postmodern, while the latter is often associated with the New Journalism (or excoriated by feminists for patriarchal sexism).[11] One knows that such labels are all but useless when it is a question of inventive, strong, and varied oeuvres like those of Coover and Mailer. All the same, it would seem safe to say that *The Executioner's Song*, the "true life novel," with its sober reporting of witnesses' accounts, could hardly be at a further remove from *The Public Burning*, with its exuberant linguistic style and exaggeration of absurdities. Yet, strangely, there is a very strong affinity between them when one looks a little closely, or not even all that closely.

For instance, each deploys extensively the metaphor of the circus, whether it is the circus emceed in Times Square by Uncle Sam in *The Public Burning* or the circus of media that compete for the story of Gilmore's final act in *The Executioner's Song*. The circus, of course, was once the circled stadium where the Romans staged, among other spectacles, executions by gladiator of condemned prisoners who had been offered the chance to fight for their lives. These are like the spectacles and festivals that Nietzsche places near the origin of punishment, at which creditors exacted what their debtors owed them in the currency of cruelty.[12] This ancient scene of punishment finds distant echoes in both novels, where the circus draws crowds for the spectacle of cruelty that is an execution.

---

11. Most famously by Kate Millett, in *Sexual Politics* (Garden City, N.Y.: Doubleday, 1970). Mailer responded to the chorus of his feminist critics in his *Prisoner of Sex* (New York: Little, Brown, 1971).

12. Friedrich Nietzsche, *On the Genealogy of Morals*, trans. Walter Kaufmann and R. J. Hollingdale (New York: Vintage, 1989), 363; see also Derrida, *DP I*, 154ff.

Indeed, in 1960 Norman Mailer had half-seriously proposed that the U.S. president just elected (John Kennedy) introduce a bill "for a New Capital Punishment," adding that the bill "would never pass, but a new idea might be alive. Nothing is more exceptional than to introduce a new idea into America."[13] In fact, this "new idea" was essentially the ancient idea of gladiatorial combat. Here is Mailer's proposal:

> I would like to see a law passed which would abolish capital
> punishment, except for those states which insisted on keeping it.
> Such states would then be allowed to kill criminals provided that the
> killing is not impersonal but personal and a public spectacle: to wit
> that the executioner be more or less the same size and weight as the
> criminal (the law could here specify the limits) and that they fight
> to death using no weapons, or weapons not capable of killing at a
> distance. Thus knives or broken bottles would be acceptable. Guns
> would not.[14]

Mailer comments that such a reform "might return us to moral responsibility," an idea that is then further elaborated, in terms that are going to be echoed in a poem he first published in 1964 with the same title, "The Executioner's Song," which fifteen years later he would give to his novel. Leaving these echoes aside until we encounter the poem in all its detail in Chapter 4, I quote the rest of the proposal, which explicitly evokes gladiators:

> The benefit of this law is that it might return us to moral
> responsibility. The killer would carry the other man's death in his
> psyche. The audience, in turn, would experience a sense of tragedy,
> since the executioners, highly trained for this, would almost always
> win. In the flabby American spirit there is a buried sadist who finds
> the bullfight contemptible—what he really desires are gladiators.
> Since nothing is worse for a country than repressed sadism, this

13. Norman Mailer, *The Presidential Papers* (New York: G. P. Putnam's Sons, 1963), 9.
14. Mailer, *The Presidential Papers*, 11.

method of execution would offer ventilation for the more cancerous
emotions of the American public. (11)

Like Nietzsche, then, Mailer understands that pleasure taken in the
other's pain—sadism—is the repressed motive of punishment. Or
as Nietzsche put it: "Without cruelty there is no festival: thus the
longest and most ancient part of human history teaches—and in
punishment there is so much that is *festive!*" (*Genealogy*, 67).

The figure of the execution circus, however, is not the only feature shared by these novels. There is also the invention of what,
on the one hand, Mailer calls "true life" and, on the other, the real
events and historical actors that Coover redeploys under the cover
of his fiction. This adherence to historical record, if only to the first
draft of history in the newspapers from which both novels cut and
paste extensively, seems calibrated by the calculations that count
down precisely to a time of death as history has recorded it. This
countdown structures each novel with a similar precision. The
structure of calculation from a sentenced, predetermined end is
also, and in general, a foundational element of conventional narrative, which plots the end from the beginning and vice versa. Both
Coover and Mailer take over this plot but, I would venture, in order
to *write over* it, by which I mean both to superimpose their writing
over it and to unwrite it or write it over, changing everything and
nothing, like Pierre Menard's *Don Quixote*. In the overwriting carried out by their respective fictions, the interest of the death penalty
plot—its circus appeal—shows up its threadbare weave throughout
the fabric of post-*Gregg* American society.

This effect is especially evident in *The Executioner's Song*, which
is not surprising, because Mailer was writing in such close prox-
imity to events the novel recounts. By eschewing, however, the
first-person subjectivism of New Journalism, which Mailer had pio-
neered in the 1960s with works like *Armies of the Night* and *Miami
and the Siege of Chicago*, *The Executioner's Song* manages a degree
of "objective" recording that may be audible or readable only at a

distance such as ours from what the novel was picking up like background noise in its recorded chronicle of Gilmore's brief life and grisly death by firing squad. A new regime of the death penalty post-*Gregg* was also ushering in the coming era of punishment, which would be characterized by mass incarceration and by the stigmatization of the criminal, especially the black criminal. It is the era that Michelle Alexander has so searingly named the New Jim Crow, when a new complex of "colorblind" laws and policies takes over the task of social control of an underclass that is made up disproportionally of persons of color.[15]

Although published more than forty years before the era that Alexander documents, Richard Wright's best-known novel, *Native Son*, can be read, with little resistance, as if addressed to this posterity. Significantly, one of the clearest moments of this prescient address comes in the form of a vision that the protagonist Bigger Thomas has in prison:

> Standing trembling in his cell, he saw a dark vast fluid image rise and float; he saw a black sprawling prison full of tiny black cells in which people lived; each cell had its stone jar of water and a crust of bread and no one could go from cell to cell and there were screams and curses and yells of suffering and nobody heard them, for the walls were thick and darkness was everywhere. Why were there so many cells in the world?[16]

It is a vision full of darkness—"dark vast fluid image" and "darkness everywhere"—but also blackness: a "black sprawling prison full of tiny black cells." The repetition of "black" vehicles a metonymy, indeed the metonymy of a metonymy: It is a black prison because it is for black people, just as they are black cells because they hold black convicts. In a 1930s Chicago that has yet to learn the code of

15. Michelle Alexander, *The New Jim Crow: Mass Incarceration in the Age of Colorblindness*, rev. ed. (New York: New Press, 2012).

16. Richard Wright, *Native Son* (New York: Perennial Classics, 1989), 457.

colorblindness, the explicit stigma of blackness is the necessary and sufficient cause of everything that happens in the novel, from the opening scene of the rat infestation that Bigger's family must regularly endure to the execution of Bigger the "black ape" (342, 422, 426, 517) that looms at the end.[17] And the "Black Belt" that divides the city restrains like a prison the movement of those forced to live within it, a condition Bigger reflects on when he is on the run from the police hunting him:

> How easy it would be for him to hide if he had the whole city
> in which to move about! They keep us bottled up here like wild
> animals, he thought. He knew that black people could not go
> outside the Black Belt to rent a flat; they had to live on their side
> of the "line." No white real estate man would rent a flat to a black
> man other than in the sections where it had been decided that black
> people might live. (314)

This is mass incarceration in a previous guise, which is also to say that mass incarceration is redlining and black belting in a later guise, the colorblind guise of the New Jim Crow.[18]

Clearly *Native Son* speaks still to American experience. And like the other novels explored here, it is a story that ends in a death sentence executed by the state. Or rather, it ends on the eve of this execution, leaving the reader, like Bigger, to imagine the end:

> He had been told by one of the guards not to worry, that "eight
> seconds after they take you out of your cell and put that black cap
> over your eyes, you'll be dead, boy." Well, he could stand that. He

---

17. On Bigger's "beastliness," see Christopher Peterson, *Bestial Traces: Race, Sexuality, Animality* (New York: Fordham University Press, 2013), chap. 1.

18. David Guest makes a similar point in a chapter on *Native Son* in his *Sentenced to Death*: Wright, he says, "depicts the [criminal justice] system as the nation's primary instrument of racial oppression in the years after slavery. Even when the statutes of the penal code disallow racial discrimination—and in 1940 they seldom did—Wright shows that the racist myths are powerful enough to make the criminal justice system take up the work of racial oppression" (87).

had in his mind a plan: he would flex his muscles and shut his eyes
and hold his breath and think of absolutely nothing while they were
handling him. And when the current struck him, it would all be
over. (533)

The novel's continued relevance or pertinence is, I would say, the
hallmark of literature, that is, of writing that goes on interpreting,
allegorizing, fictionalizing any present, like past, experience. Literature is writing that we as a reading culture—which is perhaps becoming extinct—take care of and preserve, keep available for any
and all readers (*Native Son* has not gone out of print since it was
published in 1940), and carefully restore in each and all of its original words (*Native Son* was initially issued in a Book-of-the-Month
Club censored version). But of course somewhere we believe that
such pragmatic indicators merely imply a prior judgment of the
quality called literature, which a work simply does or does not ex-
hibit. That is, works are preserved and restored because they *are* literature, rather than the other way around. Finally, however, can this
difference be decided, and doesn't it come down to the same thing?
    Yet *Native Son* perhaps excepts itself from this reasoning. This
may even be what James Baldwin sought to articulate when he positioned Wright's novel in a line of descent from *Uncle Tom's Cabin*
in his 1949 essay "Everybody's Protest Novel."[19] In a related essay
a few years later, "Many Thousands Gone," Baldwin reserves the
phrase "protest literature" for certain writing "written by Negroes,"
of which the first, and only, example given is *Native Son*.[20] Baldwin's critique of the novel is severe and argues that it essentially
fails to do what a novel should do, to "journey toward a more vast

19. "Bigger is Uncle Tom's descendant, so exactly opposite a portrait that, when the books
are placed together, it seems that the contemporary Negro novelist and the dead New England
woman are locked in a deadly embrace; the one uttering merciless exhortations, the other
shouting curses." James Baldwin, "Everybody's Protest Novel,' in *Notes of a Native Son* (Boston: Beacon, 1984), 22.
    20. Baldwin, "Many Thousands Gone," in *Notes of a Native Son*, 31.

reality" and reveal the complexity in which we can "find at once ourselves and the power that will free us from ourselves. It is this power of revelation which is the business of the novelist, this journey toward a more vast reality which must take precedence over all other claims" ("Everybody's Protest Novel," 15). But Baldwin was no doubt being unjust. He came close to admitting as much when he wrote in the aftermath of Wright's death.[21] Abdul JanMohamed, for one, protests vigorously against the dismissive label of "protest literature" and against Baldwin's critique in his own lengthy study of Wright's fiction.[22]

As I said, I did not set out to shadow recent chapters of the American death penalty or carceral regime through the pages of its literature.[23] I thus determined not to subject Wright's death penalty novel to any longer reading here. And with that decision I also dropped whatever designs I might have had on Albert Camus's famous novel *The Stranger,* except for some brief analysis of it in Chapter 1. I had come to relate these two works, not all that implausibly, and not only because Camus would become an admirer of Wright's novel, but also because their protagonists follow such similar trajectories, however different their circumstances. And like *Native Son, The Stranger* ends famously on the eve of the protagonist's execution with Meursault, the condemned man, reflecting in his cell:

21. James Baldwin, "Alas, Poor Richard," in *Nobody Knows My Name* (New York: Vintage, 1961). But Baldwin has already signaled his connection, affinity, and debt to Wright with the title of an essay about the death of his own father, "Notes of a Native Son," in a collection with the same name.

22. Abdul R. JanMohamed, *The Death-Bound Subject: Richard Wright's Archaeology of Death* (Durham, NC: Duke University Press, 2005), 39–42.

23. Had that been the aim, then the choice of fictional works examined in the following chapters would manifestly have been inadequate to the purpose. Fortunately, others, like Guest and Barton, have taken up that task and no doubt studies of American literature in the age of mass incarceration and "the new Jim Crow" will supplement their work before long.

I opened myself for the first time to the tender indifference of the world. Feeling it so much like me, so fraternal in the end, I felt that I had been happy, and that I was happy still. For everything to be fulfilled, for me to feel less alone, there remained for me to hope that there would be many spectators on the day of my execution and that they would greet me with cries of hatred.[24]

As Alice Kaplan has pointed out, *The Stranger* assumed shape out of an obsessive vision that Camus lent initially to Patrice Merseult, the protagonist of his aborted first novel *A Happy Death*. This precursor of Meursault claims "a man condemned to death was living and breathing inside him": "I see that man. He is inside me . . . He is living and breathing with me. He is afraid with me."[25] Camus's writing was born when that man condemned to death moved onto the page.

Every somewhat alert reader of Camus's famous novel understands that Meursault is condemned not because he killed the unnamed Arab man on the beach but because of his seeming indifference to the death of his mother.[26] For the Algerian writer Kamel Daoud, this injustice was the premise for his own novel published in French in 2013, *Meursault contre-enquête*, translated in English as *The Meursault Investigation*. Daoud's narrator is Haroun, the surviving younger brother of Moussa/Zoudj, "the Arab" killed by Meursault on the beach that day in 1942. In a bar in Oran, he is

24. Albert Camus, *L'étranger* (Paris: Gallimard, 1942), 183–184; my trans. Although with this ending Camus might have been nodding toward Wright's novel, there is a more likely echo of James M. Cain's 1934 potboiler *The Postman Always Rings Twice*, which also ends with the narrator, Frank Chambers, awaiting imminent execution. Like Meursault, Chambers is a murderer, but one effectively convicted for a crime he did not commit. On the relation between the two works, see Alice Kaplan, *Looking for the Stranger: Albert Camus and the Life of a Literary Classic* (Chicago: University of Chicago Press, 2016), 46–48.

25. Kaplan, *Looking for the Stranger*, 46, 234n3.

26. This "crime" is declared with the dispassionate tone of the very first, and very famous, sentences of the novel: "Today Mother died. Or maybe yesterday."

telling his story to a literary scholar come from Paris to do research on the author of the book in which Haroun's brother died and was forgotten. Here is how his recital begins:

> It happened, and everyone talked about it. People still do, but they mention only one dead man, they feel no compunction about doing that, you see, even though there were two of them, two dead men. Yes, two. Why does the other one get left out? Well, the first one was such a good storyteller, he managed to make people forget his crime, whereas the second one was a poor illiterate God created for the sole purpose, it seems, of taking a bullet and returning to dust—an anonymous person who didn't even have time to have a name.[27]

Daoud's novel goes on to shadow Camus's in ways too numerous and too complex to summarize.[28] Suffice it to say that it does something of which there may be no other examples in our literary traditions when it attaches itself, without parody or satire, to the earlier work like a version to be read between its lines. Or, as Haroun puts it,

> I'm going to do what was done in this country after Independence: I'm going to take the stones one by one from the old houses the colonists left behind, and build my own house, my own language. The murderer's words and expressions are my *vacant property*. (2; trans. modified)

I am nearly done accounting for the fictions that are taken up, or not, in this book. Its concluding chapter attempts to reflect in some general terms on literature of the death penalty, with the help

27. Kamel Daoud, *The Meursault Investigation*, trans. John Cullen (New York: Other Press, 2015), 1; trans. modified.

28. As just one index of how closely Daoud shadows (or stalks) Camus's novel, the 2014 French edition of *Meursault contre-enquête* (a first edition was published in Algeria in 2013) has exactly the same number of signs as *L'étranger*; see Alice Kaplan, "'Meursault, contre-enquête' de Kamel Daoud," in *contreligne*, June 2014, http://www.contreligne.eu/2014/06/kamel-daoud-meursault-contre-enquete/.

once again of Derrida. His 1985 essay "Before the Law" has been on this book's mind, so to speak, since its inception, but this preoccupation surfaces only briefly in Chapter 4 before providing the key articulations for a reading of Charles Baudelaire's prose poem "A Heroic Death" in Chapter 5. It is the occasion to ask again what a literary text is doing, performatively, when it comes before the law of the death penalty, but also to ask what happens to the law that has to appear before a literary work. These are the questions that all of the chapters have taken as their guides to reading each time a singular work.

1

BEGINNING WITH LITERATURE

"Why, on the death penalty, begin with literature?" asks Jacques Derrida early in the first year of his seminar on the death penalty.[1] The very formulation of the question implies this is such a surprising place to begin that it demands explanation. Why indeed speak of literature just as one is beginning to address the life-and-death issue of capital punishment? Especially if, as Derrida remarks elsewhere, one must profess oneself dumbstruck, "stupefied," by the fact that "never, *to my knowledge*, has any philosopher, *as such, in his properly philosophical discourse*, never has any philosophy *as such* contested the legitimacy of the death penalty."[2] This stupefying fact (he calls it "for me the most significant and the most stupefying—also the most stupefied—fact in the history of Western philosophy")

1. Jacques Derrida, *The Death Penalty, Volume I,* ed. Geoffrey Bennington and Thomas Dutoit, trans. Peggy Kamuf (Chicago: University of Chicago Press, 2013), 29; hereafter *DP I.*

2. Jacques Derrida and Elisabeth Roudinesco, *For What Tomorrow: A Dialogue,* trans. Jeff Fort (Stanford, Calif.: Stanford University Press, 2004), 146; see also the chapter "The Philosopher, as Such, and the Death Penalty," in Peggy Kamuf, *To Follow: The Wake of Jacques Derrida* (Edinburgh: Edinburgh University Press, 2010), 187–193.

should be a goad to undertake what "to my knowledge" no other philosopher in the tradition has done: contest the legitimacy of the death penalty with the means of properly philosophical discourse. To be sure, the effects of this goad are sensible in the seminar, in particular when Derrida goes head to head with Kant, who is positioned as the tradition's most rigorous defender of the death penalty. But even these direct confrontations with Kant's argument are relatively brief compared to the long passages devoted to close readings of texts by Victor Hugo, Maurice Blanchot, Albert Camus, Jean Genet, or even Robert Badinter, the lawyer and author of *The Execution*,[3] a narrative account of his unsuccessful defense of a famous capital case in France in the early 1970s. Of these, Hugo and Camus are widely known as vigorous and tireless opponents of the death penalty, and Badinter will long be remembered for his efforts to abolish the death penalty in France, which was accomplished while he was minister of justice in 1981.[4] Thus, although not one philosopher in the tradition is on record qua philosopher arguing against capital punishment (as if they were all loath to find fault with Socrates's reasoning in *Crito*), for at least two centuries writers and poets (and not only French ones, of course!) have not only taken strong public stands in favor of its abolition (in which they were hardly alone) but have given us literary works that work against the death penalty.

Now, in light of this stark contrast, Derrida's question—"Why, on the death penalty, begin with literature?"—starts to seem rather less surprising than at first blush. And indeed, after posing the question, he will proceed to remind us of the abolitionist strain in modern literary discourse. But he does so by way of posing a certain "hypothesis," which, he writes, "in its main features would come down to this":

---

3. Robert Badinter, *L'exécution* (Paris: Grasset, 1973).

4. See Badinter's subsequent book *L'abolition* (Paris: Librairie Arthème Fayard, 2000), which recounts the fight in the French parliament to abolish the death penalty in France.

If the history of the general possibility, of the largest territory of the
general conditions of possibility of epic, poetic, or belle-lettristic
productions (not of literature in the strict and modern sense)
supposes or goes hand in hand with the legitimacy or the legality of
the death penalty, well then, on the contrary, the short, strict, and
modern history of the institution named literature in Europe over the
last three or four centuries is contemporary with and *indissociable*
from a contestation of the death penalty, an abolitionist struggle that,
to be sure, is uneven, heterogeneous, discontinuous, but irreversible
and tending toward the worldwide as conjoined history, once again,
of literature and rights, and of *the right to literature*. (*DP I*, 30;
emphases added)

I have added emphases at two points to bring out the key articulations of this hypothesis, the points that most need to be tested or argued. First, there is the idea that the modern institution of literature
is not just contemporary with but *indissociable* from the struggle
for abolition of the death penalty. In other words, the contempo-
raneousness of these two historical currents is not contingent but
expresses some necessary relation. But what is that relation? The
second emphasized phrase, *the right to literature*, points the way
toward an answer.

Although the phrase "right to literature" is going to recur twice
more in the course of these lectures (on pages 108 and 117), it is
not in *The Death Penalty* seminar that Derrida explains how he understands it. For that, one may turn to an essay from 1993 where
he spells out this right in terms that echo closely the passage just
quoted from the seminar.

I have often found myself insisting on the necessity of distinguishing
between literature and belles-lettres or poetry. Literature is a
modern invention, inscribed in conventions and institutions that, to
retain only this trait, secure in principle its *right to say everything*.
Literature thus ties its destiny to a certain noncensure, to the space
of democratic freedom (freedom of the press, freedom of speech,

etc.). No democracy without literature; no literature without democracy. One can always want neither one nor the other, and there is no shortage of doing without them under all regimes; it is quite possible to consider neither of them to be unconditional goods and indispensable rights. But in no case can one dissociate one from the other.[5]

Manifestly, the indissociable relation posed here between literature (in the modern sense) and democracy accounts for the claim in the seminar that, as we just read, "the institution named literature in Europe over the last three or four centuries is contemporary with and *indissociable* from a contestation of the death penalty." Moreover, by glossing the right to literature as "the right to say everything" ("le droit de tout dire"), Derrida in effect prepares his later claim. But how so? How is the right to say everything necessarily associated with opposition to the death penalty?

First, it must be remarked that this right (to say everything) is not *someone*'s right but the right *of* literature *as* literature in the modern sense. Even though someone may exercise it (for example, an author), it is nevertheless not an individual's right, the way the right to vote or freely assemble are individual rights upheld (at least in principle!) in a democratic polity. To be sure, this makes this right rather anomalous, but it is just this anomaly that is recognized and protected by democratic codes of law. It is recognized and protected, for example, by boilerplate language printed on copyright pages of books that call themselves novels, novellas, short stories, or, more generically, fictions:[6] for example, "This book is a work of fiction. Names, characters, places and incidents are products of the author's imagination or used fictitiously. Any resemblance

---

5. Jacques Derrida, "Passions: 'An Oblique Offering,'" trans. David Wood, in *On the Name*, ed. Thomas Dutoit (Stanford, Calif.: Stanford University Press, 1999), 28. For another reading of these pages on "the right to say everything," see Peggy Kamuf, *Book of Addresses* (Stanford, Calif.: Stanford University Press, 2005), chap. 9, esp. 180–183.

6. And as often as not, such designations appear only in this legal disclaimer.

to actual events or locales or persons, living or dead, is entirely coincidental."[7] As we all know, such statements function formally and publicly to disclaim responsibility to "tell the truth" in the work in question. More broadly speaking, however, they invoke literature or fiction as a right of nonresponse.

Which brings us to a second remark about this right to say everything. It is also the right to say nothing, or rather the right and even the obligation not to respond to a demand to know, to divulge the hidden or unapparent, to make public what is secret. In the pages we are reading from *On the Name*, Derrida calls this the right to secrecy and acknowledges that only with literature does one encounter something resembling an unconditional respect of secrets. Morality, religion, politics, and law, as well as all disciplines of knowledge and technology, are constituted as authorities entitled to demand accounts and responses of whichever responsible subjects fall under their purview. Literary fictions, by contrast, figure a space of nonresponse to the demand to know and therefore a reserve of unconditional secrecy. (Even writers deluded enough to believe they know and can therefore divulge secrets of their characters or the events that happen in their fictional worlds are constrained by the radical dissociation between author and character to do no more than invent more fiction when pressed to so—for example, on Sunday morning radio interviews.)

To illustrate this right to nonresponse that literary fiction arrogates to itself, one might recall another text of Derrida's in which he reads and interprets in a nearly exhaustive manner a short prose poem of Baudelaire's, "Counterfeit Money."[8] It is a simple enough story: As they are leaving a tobacco shop, two friends encounter a

---

7. Although it is, precisely, boilerplate and thus hardly an original source, this language is in fact from the copyright page of Stephen King's *The Green Mile: The Complete Serial Novel* (New York: Pocket Books, 1996).

8. See Jacques Derrida, *Given Time, I: Counterfeit Money*, trans. Peggy Kamuf (Chicago: University of Chicago Press, 1992).

poor man holding out his cap. Both the narrator and his friend put coins in the cap, but the friend is more generous. Noticing this, the narrator is prompted to reflect aloud that his friend is right to be so generous since there is no greater pleasure than causing surprise, meaning the poor man's surprise at such a windfall. Whereupon the friend calmly replies that the coin he gave the other was counterfeit. This sends the narrator off on some wild speculations about what good fortune or misfortunes might befall the poor man with his counterfeit coin, until the friend shatters the reverie by repeating the narrator's own words back to him to the effect that there is "no sweeter pleasure than to surprise a man by giving him more than he hopes for." Now the narrator is led to excoriate his friend in his mind for having thought "to do a good deed while at the same time making a good deal." The story concludes with the narrator condemning the other for doing evil not out of malice but out of stupidity.

Derrida, as I said, reads this short fiction in an almost exhaustive fashion, virtually word for word, drawing from it countless connections to his own reflections in his book on the gift and giving in their supposed distinction from exchange and economy. But for our present purpose what is most telling in this interpretive performance is the very succinct question Derrida asks about the friend's truthfulness when he claims to have given the poor man a counterfeit coin. The narrator never wonders whether his friend was in fact giving him, the narrator, a truthful account of his action, even though this friend has just confessed to passing counterfeit money. "What if," Derrida asks, "with the simulacrum of a confession, he were passing off true money as false?"[9] This possibility would reverse the whole moralizing direction of the narrative, making of the narrator rather than his friend the stupid, credulous, and self-righteous one of the two. The point is, however, that this question

9. Derrida, *Given Time*, 96.

can never receive any response that would decide once and for all what was counterfeit, who was duped, and who was generous. And this nonresponse to questions that seek to know is emblematic of what Derrida calls "the secret *of* literature: what literary fiction tells us about the secret, about the (non-) truth of the secret, but also a secret whose possibility assures the possibility of literature" (153). Or, to put it in more paradoxical terms: "The readability of the text is structured by the unreadability of the secret, that is, by the inaccessibility of a certain intentional meaning or of a wanting-to-say in the consciousness of the characters and *a fortiori*, in that of the author who remains, *in this regard*, in a situation analogous to that of the reader" (152).[10]

This inaccessibility, unreadability, or inviolability of the secret, writes Derrida, "depends on nothing other than the altogether bare device of being-two-to-speak" (153). Baudelaire's tale is constructed by means of this altogether bare device. Being-two-to-speak, however, is not as such a condition of literature, of course, but a general one. Derrida points to this general condition when he remarks: "to the extent . . . that *there is dialogue*, there can be lie and inviolate secret" (151). What the literary work exposes, however, is the inviolability of a secret that no interpretation, investigation, or interrogation can overcome. Rather, it is and must be unconditionally respected, which, as we have already noted, sets literature apart from all discourses of knowledge and all forms of social authority (religion, morality, politics, law, science) that act to penetrate secrecy in their authorized, truth-seeking capacity.

It is this distinctive feature of literature that can take us back to our questions: How is the "right to say everything"—and therefore also nothing, nonresponse—indissociable from opposition to the

---

10. For wide-ranging treatments of Derrida's thinking of secrecy, see Charles Barbour, *Derrida's Secret: Perjury, Testimony, Oath* (Edinburgh: Edinburgh University Press, 2017), esp. chap. 2; and Ginette Michaud, *Tenir au secret (Derrida, Blanchot)* (Paris: Éditions Galilée, 2006).

death penalty? And once again: "Why, on the death penalty, begin with literature?"

Another fictional text can take us further into these questions. At the beginning of the second part of Camus's crime and punishment novel *The Stranger*, the main character and narrator Meursault describes his interrogations by the examining magistrate after his arrest. There are in particular two questions to which the magistrate seeks responses from the narrator: First, why did he pause before firing four more times into the body of the unnamed Arab man he has already gunned down? And second, did he love his mother? The first question is put repeatedly, and each time Meursault makes no reply:

> "Why did you pause between the first and second shot?" Once again I could see the red sand and feel the burning of the sun on my forehead. But this time I didn't answer. . . .
>
> "Why, why did you shoot at a body that was on the ground?" Once again I didn't know how to answer. . . .
>
> "Why? You must tell me. Why?" Still I didn't say anything.[11]

To the other question, "he asked me if I loved my mother," Meursault does respond, but his laconic reply, "Yes, like everybody," sets off a little crisis in the machinery of justice: "The court clerk who up to this point was typing steadily on his machine must have hit the wrong keys because he got mixed up and had to go back" (103–104). These nonresponses drape a silence over two discrete events—the death of the Arab man, the death of the mother—that, though unrelated, are going to communicate secretly as, precisely, secrets, that is, as holes in knowledge that the prosecutor, jury, and judge are going to have to fill in however they might in order to ground their judgment of guilt. They thus open up the two gaps in Meursault's account that will finally condemn him to death.

Camus's novel is almost exactly divided between its two parts,

---

11. Albert Camus, *L'étranger* (Paris: Gallimard, 1942), 104; my trans.

the first of which famously begins "Today, Mother died" and ends with Meursault's killing of the Arab man, the same two events that the second part will reconstruct, examine, and pass judgment on through the formalities of interrogation and trial. Although the novel is continuously narrated in the same first person, this two-part structure is nevertheless able to display the incommensurability between an experience of events and their narration. The novel thus positions its readers as witnesses to that incommensurability, to the chasm it creates, into which Meursault is cast when summoned to respond before the law. But it also highlights a kind of secret that Meursault does not so much harbor as suffer or undergo when he is pressed to respond by the law's questions: "Why? You must tell me. Why?" "Did you love your mother?" The secret is inviolable even or especially by Meursault, which does not prevent the representatives of the law lined up against him from filling the hole in knowledge with their judgment. When Meursault reflects on the "ridiculous disproportion" between the contingency of the judgment against him, which might have been altogether different, and the implacable, machine-like necessity of his death sentence once it is pronounced (165), he throws into relief the only certainty established by his trial: the certainty of its sentence.

If Camus's novel registers a strong protest against capital punishment, it is also because it adopts a device initially tested by Victor Hugo in 1829 in *The Last Day of a Condemned Man*: a first-person account of life after a death sentence. It is not, to be sure, a complex device, but it can pack a wallop when the reader is led to identify, as inevitably one is, with an "I" who is also me, any or every me. For as Derrida will come to argue clearly by the end of *The Death Penalty I*, what has to arouse the most vigorous condemnation of the condemnation to death is that it kills the very principle of life, which is the incalculability of a future, of the event that comes from an unknowable other. Through its calculation of date, time, place, and means of death, capital punishment would seem, Derrida argues, to put an end to the finitude the condition of which is the incalculability of "my death." As such, the death penalty lives on the phantasm of mastering "my death" by calculating it.

It is probably not insignificant that, when Derrida pauses to ask "Why, on the death penalty, begin with literature?", he is preparing to read the beginning of Jean Genet's 1948 novel *Our Lady of the Flowers*. To be sure, this is a work that, in so many ways, seizes and exercises the right to literature, the right to say anything. But what will be highlighted in Derrida's reading is another dimension of the indissociable connection between literature and contestation of the death penalty, namely a "desacralization" as performed by profane, secular, post-Enlightenment—modern—literature but also by abolitionist discourse to the extent that that discourse "breaks with the scene and the authority of Exodus and divine judgment" (*DP I*, 30). In *Our Lady of the Flowers*, this break registers as a transfer of elements from the narrative of Christ's execution and resurrection to the executed heroes of this new evangelist who is Jean Genet. Throughout Genet's work, there is, notes Derrida, "a performance of anti-Christian Christian iconoclasm, of perjury and abjuration fascinated with the very thing that it turns into literature the way one might say to turn something into a mockery" (*DP I*, 32). This literature, in other words, comes out of a turn at once toward and away from the martyred Christ, who was put to death— like Socrates, al-Hallaj, and Joan of Arc[12]—for speech acts claiming to testify to a transcendence other than the one sanctioned by theologico-political authority. Modern literature—not just Genet's but Genet's in an exemplary manner—comes out of this desacralizing turn that, like the great executed martyrs, signals to another transcendence—or quasi transcendence. It inherits heretical speech but, in its modern institution, founds no doctrine of belief. In coming under the protection of its disclaimed responsibility as fiction,

---

12. Derrida begins the first year of his death penalty seminar by convoking these four figures put to death by the state for religious crimes.

this new heretic cannot be put to death. And such an exemption or immunity, at least in principle, is unconditional, which carves out for modern literature a singular place from which to view the death penalty as well as societies that carry it out—and to *respond* from out of its disclaimed responsibility.

Derrida quickly sketches all of this through the reading of the first two pages of *Our Lady of the Flowers*, which he intercuts with two long annotations from the Gospel of John (or Jean, like Jean Genet, if one is speaking French). The motif that crosses between the two texts, the biblical and the heretical, is the word and the thing *bandages*, one of the first words of Genet's novel: "Weidmann appeared before you in a five o'clock edition, his head swaddled in white bandages [*bandelettes*] . . ." Derrida is going to wind and unwind these bandages through two passages in the Gospel when John records and testifies to the death and resurrection of Jesus. In the first of these, the dead body of Jesus is wound in "linen clothes" (*bandelettes*) and spices. In the second, John recounts Mary Magdalene's discovery of the empty tomb of Jesus and Simon Peter's seeing the abandoned linen clothes in the tomb. Derrida bids us to remark how Genet has wrapped these holy bandages around the head of the multiple murderer Eugène Weidmann, who was publicly guillotined in June 1939 and has taken over the signs of glory and transcendence. But Derrida is also going to insert an important parenthesis into his commentary on this transfer from the biblical story to the heretical literary one. Commenting on the scene at the empty tomb, from John 20: 1–18, he writes:

> The bandages do indeed *appear*; they are there all of a sudden;
> they leap into the light: it is a *phenomenon* that seems to signify,
> that makes a sign as in a vision. The time of this phenomenon of
> the bandages, their moment in the story and in the process is very
> remarkable (and if we had the leisure to do so, if it were the subject
> of the seminar, we would meditate on this time of the bandages

as the lodging made ready for literature, for an ascension without ascension, an elevation without elevation, an imminent but not yet accomplished resurrection, etc.). *(DP I, 34)*

Literature, then, would come to be lodged in this "time of the bandages" between death and resurrection, beyond life yet still there, still appearing as Jesus appears to Mary Magdalene when she turns away from the mouth of the empty tomb and sees a man she at first takes to be a gardener (John 20:14–15). Like the bandages, literature signals as trace of an absence and in a time suspended between all the modes of presence, like Jesus when he appears to Mary and warns *noli me tangere*. Derrida flexes long, rhythmical phrases to gloss this ghostly "time of the bandages," for example: "These bandages, the second apparition of the bandages, the untied bandages, abandoned near Christ's tomb, are going to signify that Christ is not dead, that he is no longer dead: he will have been dead; to be sure, he died, but he is not yet resuscitated, not yet elevated: he is still there . . ." *(DP I, 34)*, and then a little later:

> This singular instant, Christ's being-there without being-there, this *Dasein* that is not a *Da-sein*, this *Fort / Da-sein* of Christ who is dead but not dead, who is living dead [*mort vivant*], who is resuscitated but not yet risen, who is here without being here, here but there, over there (*fort, jenseits*), who is already beyond without yet being beyond, in the beyond . . . this singular moment that does not belong to the ordinary unfolding of time . . . this time without time . . .
> *(DP I, 37)*

Like John the Evangelist's, Jean the novelist's story lifts the figure of the executed man in a movement of elevation or ascension. According to the Gospel, it is the lingering shade of Jesus who announces his ascension: "Jesus saith unto her, Touch me not; for I am not yet ascended to my Father: but go to my brethren, and say unto them, I ascend unto my Father, and your Father; and to my God, and your God" (John 20:17). As for Weidmann, it is Jean the evange-

list who conjures "his secret glory" and "his future glory" but who
also reports the words of the condemned man: "As for their death,
need I tell you about it? For all of them it will be the death of the
one who, when he learned of his from the jury, merely mumbled
in a Rhenish accent 'I'm already beyond that' (Weidmann)" (qtd. in
DP I, 37–38).

The story turns into literature—and also perhaps mockery—
in the spacing of phrases that have the form "X without X." This
formula recurs at least three times in these pages where Derrida
is pursuing our question "Why, on the death penalty, begin with
literature?" Most pointedly, the syntax "X without X" is twice ap-
posed to literature in the parentheses where Derrida, as we saw,
lodges it in the time of the bandages, "the lodging made ready for
literature, for an ascension without ascension, an elevation without elevation . . ." This "without" between the repetitions does not
signal a cancelation; it is not privative but has instead the effect of
suspending the positing force of language. As such, "X without X"
names literature's act of positing without positing and of reference
without referent.[13] It names the act of fiction, in a word, this heresy
that every would-be democracy is obliged to lodge within/without
itself. No democracy without literature, in other words, no democracy without this without, without its transcendence without transcendence, "an ascension without ascension, an elevation without
elevation." Jean the evangelist brings the good news of this other
transcendence as poetic performance.

Unlike Hugo's *The Last Day of a Condemned Man*, Genet's
novels make no claim to be "nothing other than argument, direct or
indirect as one wishes, for the abolition of the death penalty."[14] Men
like Weidmann, men sentenced to death for the worst crimes, are

---

13. See Jacques Derrida, "The Double Session," in *Dissemination*, trans. Barbara Johnson
(Chicago: University of Chicago Press, 1981), 219.
14. Victor Hugo, 1832 Preface to *Le dernier jour d'un condamné*, in *Écrits sur la peine de
mort* (Arles: Actes Sud, 1979), 9; my trans.

glorious heroes for Genet's narrators and characters, who dream
about, sanctify, and desire them. They are the martyrs of this author's "Christian anti-Christian iconoclasm," as Derrida calls it.
These are not innocents wrongly accused; they have not repented
or made amends. Like Weidmann, they all can say "I am already beyond that." It is around this figure that Genet's novels are wound
like bandages that turn the basest degradation into incomparable
poetry. And as such they work against a capital punishment regime
that must pretend to ignore its own perverse effects. Genet himself
professes that the *peine de mort*, the death penalty and the pain
of death, which is the death of the other, is that without which he
would not have written. His first two published writings, the long
poem *The Man Condemned to Death* and *Our Lady of the Flowers*,
are dedicated to Maurice Pilorge, a convicted murderer guillotined
in Rennes, France, in February 1939. Nine years later, the dedication of *Our Lady of the Flowers* reads: "Without Maurice Pilorge
whose death is still poisoning my life I would never have written
this book. I dedicate it to his memory."[15] As if to say that the book,
with its poetic reveries, fantasies, dreams, and fictions within fictions, was drawn from the poison injected by the other's death on
the scaffold.

An emblem of this transformation might be found in several lines
Derrida quotes from Genet's next novel, *The Miracle of the Rose*.
Once again the narrator is conjuring up the glory that awaits the
executed one, a glory to which the narrator aspires:

> The purest of them who received that death felt placed, within
> themselves and on their severed head, the amazing and secret crown,
> studded with jewels wrested from the darkness of the heart. Each of
> them knew that the moment his head fell into the basket of sawdust
> and was lifted out by the ears by an assistant whose role seems to

15. Derrida quotes this dedication, *DP I,* 33. For a detailed account—and rectification
of Genet's fictionalized account—of Genet's friendship with Pilorge, see François Sentein,
L'assassin et son bourreau: Jean Genet et Maurice Pilorge (Arles: Actes Sud, 1999).

me strange indeed, his heart would be gathered up by fingers gloved
with modesty and carried off in a youngster's bosom, adorned like a
spring festival. (qtd. in *DP I*, 39)

Genet is here doing just what he is describing: adorning the heart
of the other as he tucks it into the bosom of language. The barbaric
ritual of execution thus becomes prelude to a spring festival that,
unlike the public beheading, has no witnesses other than this poetic
image that forever suspends its referent in its performance.

These works of Genet nevertheless share at least one feature
with Hugo's so very different novel, *The Last Day of a Condemned
Man*. Both of them invoke the right to literature with its attendant
unconditional secrecy. When Hugo appends a long preface to his
novel three years after its first publication, however, he more or
less dismisses or disowns the fictional appearance of his text, which
had been originally published without author's name in 1829,
when France was still ruled by the Restoration monarchy. One of
the first gestures of the preface Hugo wrote three years later for
a new edition of the novel, then, is to affix his name to a text that
had appeared anonymously under a nondemocratic regime.[16] Free
to speak his name and, in his name, his opposition to the death
penalty, Hugo all but discards the fiction, which he qualifies as an
"innocent and candid literary form."

> At the time this book was published, the author did not deem it
> appropriate to say everything he thought. He preferred to wait
> until it was understood and to see if it would be. It was. Today
> the author can unmask the political idea, the social idea, that he
> wanted to popularize beneath this innocent and candid literary
> form. He therefore declares or rather he confesses openly that *The
> Last Day of a Condemned Man* is nothing other than an argument

---

16. The so-called July Monarchy installed in 1830 was hardly a full-fledged democracy,
but it did cancel many forms of censorship in place under the deposed regime of Charles X.

[*plaidoyer*], direct or indirect as one wishes, for the abolition of the death penalty.[17]

This long, argumentative preface thus comes to supplement the fictional text so that together they configure something like the indissociable relation of literature in the modern sense and the contestation of the death penalty. Probably no one more insistently than Victor Hugo sought to shape that relation, which is one reason Derrida engages with his writings again and again in *The Death Penalty*. This continued engagement brings out the particular form that Hugo gave to abolitionist discourse, especially its appeal to a higher, divine law, which is the law of Christ. It also foregrounds its reliance, as principle of its opposition, on the notion of a sanctity of life and its condemnation of cruelty. Hugo, of course, did not solely invent these arguments; he also inherited them, like the Christian belief that underlies and permeates all his writings on the death penalty. But he powerfully articulated these themes in a style that is never dispassionate, detached, or, as we say, objective. Instead, there is always a *writer* at work against the death penalty, whether those writings are called novels, poems, plays, or some presumed nonliterary genre—preface, speech to the National Assembly, courtroom argument, or letter to the newspapers. I say "presumed nonliterary" because what is presumed here is precisely the modern institution of literature as fiction that declares itself as such before the law. But one may (and indeed one must) read Hugo's work as also taking over a practice of writing that antedates this institution, a practice by which literature is wed to the abolitionist cause not just through its fictions or "literature" in the modern sense but also, even first of all, through the force it musters *in general* in writing against the death penalty, in the premodern sense of literature as belles lettres. Hugo, and this is not surprising, is thus on the cusp of the shift from the belle-lettristic to the modern, democratic institu-

---

17. Hugo, *Écrits sur la peine de mort*, 8–9.

tion of literature, and the most telling sign of this is the eloquence he brings to bear in the abolitionist cause.

In this regard, Derrida isolates a very telling sentence from an 1862 letter Hugo wrote to an abolitionist leader in Geneva: "Writers of the eighteenth century destroyed torture; writers of the nineteenth, I have no doubt, will destroy the death penalty" (qtd. in *DP I*, 102). Hugo is here identifying his forebears, "writers of the eighteenth century," whose writings destroyed torture (think of Voltaire, in particular). In his commentary, Derrida fastens on the repetition of "destroyed"/"will destroy" in Hugo's pithy formulation and seeks out its connection to writers, writing, and to "what in Europe is called literature."

> It is a question of *destroying* the discursive and other mechanisms,
> the supports, phantasms, and opinions, the drives, the conscious
> or semi-conscious or unconscious representations, that work to
> legitimate the death penalty; and this presupposes a certain type
> of writing, of public speech, and of a certain treatment of language
> (national and international) that has a privileged tie to what in
> Europe is called literature, as well as to those citizens who have more
> or less broken with citizenship, who are sometimes ready . . . to
> engage in certain acts of civil disobedience, to those citizens of the
> world who are called writers. (*DP I*, 102–103)

Soldering the links implicit in Hugo's assertion, Derrida arrives at the privileged tie to literature and to a "certain treatment of language" presupposed by the called-for destruction of the death penalty. He bids us to think about this: how "a certain type of writing"—literature in the broadest sense—*works against* the death penalty, as its destruction—if not its deconstruction. Between brackets, he comments thus:

> This word "destroy," used with insistence and deliberately twice,
> signifies clearly that it is a question of something other than a simple
> legislative decision or even of an institutional or constitutional,
> constituting, act: it is a question, I don't dare say of deconstructing

but in any case of destroying, of attacking, through writing, by
speaking and by writing publicly, it is a question of attacking the
foundations or the presuppositions alleged by the law or by public
opinion wherever the bases of this law or the underpinnings of
this public opinion, this *doxa*, or this orthodoxy uphold the death
penalty. (*DP I*, 102)

Derrida is going to examine under a very close lens the right of
the writer to write and speak publicly against what is still the law
and thus to act against the law. He shows that for Hugo, and for the
filiation of great French writers "from Voltaire to Chateaubriand and
to Hugo," this right is a sacred one that they give themselves

to make the law above the laws, to make themselves the
representatives of eternal justice above law and thus of divine justice.
But to make the law, to invent a new law, here, is simply to appeal to
a divine law, to a divine justice that has *already* spoken, a law older
than they and more ancient than men, a law that must be *invented*
but in the sense of being discovered or found, the way one speaks
of the invention of the body of Christ to mean the discovery of his
unlocatable body; the writer, therefore, does not perform new laws;
he does not invent or produce a new code of law except by listening,
by knowing how to listen in his heart to a divine law that already
speaks. (*DP I*, 108)

This idea of the writer's sacred right is hardly Hugo's invention;
indeed, there is no possible invention—in the other, more ordinary
sense of the term—when everything returns finally to God and was
already spoken by Him. This is the largest issue Derrida has with the
example of Hugo's abolitionist discourse and a reason, no doubt, he
does not dare call its destruction a deconstruction, for it stops short,
considerably short, of taking apart the theologico-political scaffold-
ing that holds the institution of capital punishment in place, which is
the place of the hyphen articulating the one within the other.[18]

18. On this hyphen, see *DP I*, 22–25, *passim*.

All of which leaves the question of a right to literature that does not return to God as its inventor and guarantor. As I said, this right is not discerned to individuals so much as it is claimed by an act performed under the license of literature in the modern sense. Perhaps, however, in this wholly modern, post-Enlightenment, post-Revolutionary, dare I say, *democratic* sense, literature is another kind of "God," but, if it were possible, a god without sovereignty, without power, without *Gewalt*, thus a god without god, or to recall the earlier phrases Derrida elicited from his reading of Genet, a transcendence without transcendence, "an ascension without ascension, an elevation without elevation." Literature, an impossible name of a powerless god.

This repeated syntax of "X without X" could take us, through Derrida's reading of his work, to Blanchot and, in this context, to his 1948 essay "Literature and the Right to Death," to which the fourth session of *The Death Penalty I* is largely devoted.[19] These pages are dense with long quotations from Blanchot's somewhat forbidding essay, which even Derrida, or perhaps especially Derrida as one of Blanchot's most persistent and probing readers, hesitates to align either for or against the death penalty, a punishment that is invoked here in its most emblematic form for any Frenchman or Frenchwoman: the massive guillotining of those summarily judged to be *ennemis publics* by the authorities of the Terror, the original terror of the French Revolution.

I mentioned at the beginning of this chapter that *The Death Penalty I* seminar invokes the phrase "right to literature" three times, the first of which I have already glossed. Another place this phrase occurs is here in the fourth session, in the course of the reading of Blanchot's "Literature and the Right to Death." Having aligned

---

19. On this syntax in Blanchot, see Derrida, *Parages*, ed. John P. Leavey (Stanford, Calif.: Stanford University Press, 2011), 76–78; and in relation to Kant's Third Critique, see Jacques Derrida, "Parergon," in *The Truth in Painting*, trans. Geoffrey Bennington and Ian McLeod (Chicago: University of Chicago Press, 1987).

in a compelling way and in opposite corners Hugo's discourse on the sacredness of the right to life with the "right to death" named in Blanchot's title, Derrida remarks how "the simultaneity, the synchrony, the concurrence of two great discourses, of two great irreconcilable axiomatics (a humanism of the Enlightenment [i.e., Hugo] and its opposite)" also concurs in making it a question of rights and of a "right to . . ." There follows from this a passage that is tightly articulated around this phrase "the right to," either to death or to literature, the one or the other, the one as the other. I quote it at some length:

> And it is always around the idea of right, of human rights. For if one wants to sharpen the intention of Blanchot's text, and the singular, though frightening, terrifying, properly terrorizing beauty of its title, one must clearly understand that the right to death signifies the right to accede to death (to think it, to open oneself to it, to cross its limit) both by exposing oneself to losing it, or even by giving it to oneself [*en se la donnant*] (suicide) and by giving it [*en la donnant*] in putting to death or inflicting the death penalty. It is the right to kill oneself, to be killed, or to kill: to accede to death by exceeding natural life, biological or so-called animal life. Death is not natural. And this right that is the condition of literature, the condition in the sense of the element, the *situation* of literature, this right is not a right among others. It is both the right that gives birth to literature as such, but also the law that gives birth to the law itself. There is no law or right that would not be or imply a right to death. Literature is what would think this right of right, this right to right, and this revolutionary right poses the right to literature. (*DP I*, 117)

What is "frightening" and "terrifying" when Blanchot's intention is sharpened like this is the dissolve that happens between the origin or "birth" of literature and the "birth" of law when each is granted the right to death: to put to death, to take a life, as we say, to accede to death, or simply to die, although there is nothing simple about it, as Blanchot also recalls when he writes and repeats several times in this essay, "death is the impossibility of dying." But this same impossibility gives rise or gives birth (and Derrida under-scores birth when he writes that it is "both the right that *gives birth to* literature as such, but also the law that *gives birth to* the law itself") to the law that executes a death penalty, for example (but this is the exemplary example of execution by the law, the force of law). Because Blanchot's essay inscribes literature, in the most general sense, within the dialectical "work of the negative"—which Derrida asserts is a "correct and necessary" reading of this text from 1948—it has to give one pause as to the leverage it provides *against* the death penalty. Indeed, it gives one far more than just pause, since this famous essay aligns the right to literature with the right to death delivered by the exemplary instrument of modern capital punishment, namely, the guillotine under the Revolutionary Terror. The writer, writes Blanchot, "sees himself in the Revolution."[20] The "literature that contemplates itself in revolution," and above all in the Revolutionary Terror, is born, in effect, from the same bed as the death imposed and executed by the death penalty. "Revolutionary action," Blanchot writes, "is in every respect analogous to action as embodied in literature: the passage from nothing to everything, the affirmation of the absolute as event, and of every event as absolute" (320). Blanchot gives only a slight nod toward the instrument of punishment, properly so called, and toward the punishment called capital. It is when he notes, almost by preterition, that "Death under the Terror is *not simply punishment* for seditionaries, but, as the unavoidable, in some sense desired lot of everyone, it appears to be the very operation of freedom in free men" (320). Which means that not only is it not simply punishment, but also it is not punishment at all, since it is "in some sense [the] desired lot of everyone" and thus the fulfillment of a universal desire, which is to give oneself death, in other words, to negate everything and to negate that nega-tion of everything called death, in an act of pure freedom. At which point we may well need Derrida's reminder to recall endlessly "the

20. Maurice Blanchot, "Literature and the Right to Death," in *The Work of Fire*, trans. Char-lotte Mandell (Stanford, Calif.: Stanford University Press, 1995), 321.

properly terrifying and sinister resonances and connotations of this terrorist, terrorizing thinking of literature, of this literature as Terror" (*DP I*, 117).

A fuller analysis of Derrida's reading of this essay, and of how it inflects the seminar's general preoccupation with the indissociable link between literature (in the modern, post-Revolutionary sense) and the death penalty, would have to follow it through a counterbalancing or countervailing turn, where other motifs and threads are aligned, ones that balance out or even contradict the "terrorizing thinking of literature" as something like a general, unlimited death penalty as the ultimate freedom of literature (cf. *DP I*, 117–120). One can reread for oneself this counterbalancing act in the seminar, when Derrida checks a potentially unjust reading—"I would be unjust if at this point I abandoned the reading and the terrible diagnosis aimed at or against this text"—and refuses "to condemn it to death, to the death it demands" (*DP I*, 117).

One should not, I believe, hear mere metaphor in this refusal to condemn to death *a text* and a text like this—or like any other that invokes and is given the right to literature. On the contrary, it is the right to literature that reserves or preserves the reason one can always find *not to be unjust*, the reason to suspend, stay, or cancel a death penalty—and we call that a pardon. This is not calculative reason but a *reason*, a *possible impossible* reason that begins by, as one says in French, *donner raison à l'autre*, in an expression where *reason* is also and at once *right*, where giving reason to the other gives him/her/it right, says "yes, you're right," and you have the right to have reason given to your right to say, which must also be always your right to literature. "No democracy without literature; no literature without democracy."[21]

This figure that is not a metaphor of condemning to death a text

<hr/>

21. Elsewhere Derrida has adjusted this slogan: "no deconstruction without democracy, no democracy without deconstruction." Jacques Derrida, *Politics of Friendship*, trans. George Collins (London: Verso, 1997), 105.

(e.g., Blanchot's text) made me think, as I was looking for my con-
clusion, of a passage from the seminar that is very near *its* conclu-
sion, just a page before the end of the last session. It is not this ultimate or penultimate position that brought it to mind, however, but
rather the *figure* of a door or a window that has been closed once
and for all, that has been, as one can also say in French, *condamné*,
condemned. This figure of a condemned door or window stands
for all the other possible figures of the condemnation-to-death. It
is in such figures that the death penalty, "some death penalty," will
survive, no doubt, for, as Derrida avers:

> Other figures will be found for it; other figures will be invented for
> it, other turns in the condemnation to death, and it is this rhetoric
> beyond rhetoric that we are taking seriously here. We are taking
> seriously here all that is condemned whether it be a life or a door or
> a window . . . (*DP I*, 282)

What is this "rhetoric beyond rhetoric" that Derrida says he takes seriously? It is, I would venture, where figures and so-called metaphors
become the reserve of presumed proper meaning. Where one can
condemn a life just as one condemns a door or a window and vice
versa. There proper sense is suspended from figural meaning—and,
once again, vice versa. It is where, it is there, that literature-to-come
can engage with every figure in which the death penalty survives. If
literature still has a future, if literature is literature-to-come, then it
inherits with its right all the figures of that right to death as death
penalty that Blanchot names. It inherits them, which is to say, the
literature-to-come comes also from or as the past that, as William
Faulkner said, is "not even past."

Let us stop there, with Faulkner as one of the proper and exemplary names of literature.

2

ORWELL'S EXECUTION

It may seem strange that certain uses of "execution," "to execute," and "executed" have managed to set themselves apart sharply from the other meanings these words commonly have, uses that let us speak of intentions, plans, policies, instructions, commands, orders, wills, operations, offices, laws, functions, designs, and all manner of things to be executed (or not) that are not human beings subject to the death penalty. The *OED*, for example, when it gets to this particular meaning of the verb "to execute" ("6. To inflict capital punishment upon; to put to death in pursuance of a sentence") among all the other possible uses, wonders how such an odd sense could have taken hold, as it did very early in the development of English and related languages: "It is not quite clear whether these uses [in the sense of "to put to death in pursuance of a sentence"], which occur early in French and medieval Latin, were merely developed, or whether they partly represent the etymological notion of Latin *exsequi* 'to pursue to the end.'" The dictionary's remark tries to retrieve the semantic anomaly within the net of etymology but leaves out of its account that this is the only use of the verb in the many surveyed that can take a personal direct object: to execute *someone*. The strangeness, then, is this transitivity of execution, whose object is always a person to be pursued "to the end." The anomaly apparently disappears when the elided formula is restored: It is not a person but a *sentence*, the sentence of death, that is executed, in other words, carried or followed out to the end—*ex+sequī*. Yet the sentence is such that no difference survives between it and the individual so sentenced when the one can be executed, pursued to the end, only in the (end of the) person of the other.

These reflections are a way of easing into the very large question of the witness to the execution of a death sentence and, more precisely, the question of literature as witness. The question is a large and important one because, for there to be execution of a death sentence, properly so called, a witness must be present. The witness in principle is there as a third party who does not take part in the act other than to see that it has been carried out as ordered by some sovereign authority. This witness is thus the agent of that "seeing-punish [*voir-punir*]" that Derrida calls "essential to punishment, to the right to punish as right-to-see-punish(ed)."[1] In forging this double infinitive, he is setting out a reservation vis-à-vis Michel Foucault's famous argument in *Discipline and Punish* that in the modern era physical punishment tends toward the erasure of its "great spectacle." Derrida's reservation concerns, among other things, a "technical, tele-technical, or even televisual complication of seeing, or even a virtualization of visual perception," which Foucault leaves out of his account of the disappearance of the public spectacle of punishment.[2] (As we will discuss in Chapter 3, Robert Coover's novel *The Public Burning* stages a spectacular reversal of

---

1. Jacques Derrida, *The Death Penalty, Volume I*, ed. Geoffrey Bennington and Thomas Dutoit, trans. Peggy Kamuf (Chicago: University of Chicago Press, 2013), 43; hereafter *DP I*.

2. By "tele-technical complication of seeing," Derrida has in mind, for example, film as medium for projecting scenes of execution and refers specifically to *True Crime*, a 1999 film directed by and starring Clint Eastwood. *DP I*, 49.

this "de-spectacularization.") At its core, however, the right-to-see-punish(ed) and the essential visibility of capital punishment set in place the irreducible role of the witness, which Derrida formulates as follows:

> By definition, in essence, by vocation, there will never have been any invisibility for a legal putting to death, for an application of the death penalty; there has never been, on principle, a secret or invisible execution for this verdict. The spectacle and the spectator are required. The state, the polis, the whole of politics, the co-citizenry—itself or mediated through representation—must attend and attest, it must testify publicly that death was dealt or inflicted, it must *see die* [voir mourir] the condemned one. . . . This act of witnessing—the state as witness of the execution and witness of itself, of its own sovereignty, of its own almightiness—this act of witnessing must be visual: an eye witness. (*DP I*, 3–4)

With this act of definition ("By definition . . ."), Derrida specifies "death penalty" and distinguishes it from other acts of so-called legal killing that a sovereign authorizes itself to commit, acts that may or may not be witnessed by third parties, that may or may not have the public visibility—"the spectator and the spectacle"—that the execution of a death sentence requires.[3] This is not to say that such acts are going to be left out of account in the course of the seminar; Derrida will indeed caution that, even were universal abolition of the death penalty to be achieved one day, the penalty of death would not have come to an end.[4] The sovereign state would still be a "killing state."[5] What is in question, then, is something like

---

3. On such extrajudicial executions, see David Wills, "Drone Penalty," *SubStance* 43, no. 2 (2014): 174–192.

4. "It will always be vain to conclude that the universal abolition of the death penalty, if it comes about one day, means the effective end of any death penalty" (*DP I*, 282).

5. The phrase is taken from *The Killing State: Capital Punishment in Law, Politics, and Culture*, ed. Austin Sarat (Oxford: Oxford University Press, 2001).

the proper trait of the concept of the death penalty, at least in principle, and this is the trait of visibility or nonsecrecy before a witness.

Perhaps, however, the properness of this trait starts to tremble when the witness is borne in poetic or literary form, or simply when it is consigned to a text, that is, to a set of *sealed* traces. By "sealed," I mean at once signed or sealed by the singular experience of the witness and sealed up in some reserve, nonmanifest. Testimony, as Derrida has argued elsewhere, is always sealed in this double sense at least. First, a witness always testifies to a singular act of witnessing, to what she or he alone saw, heard, understood, and so forth of what took place. Second, precisely because it has to be singular, because no one can testify in the place of another, the disclosed testimony is also withdrawn or enclosed, struck with a seal of secrecy that even the witness himself or herself cannot lift. Moreover, the seal of testimony—what signals it as what is called testimony—is that it is not proof. Testimony is always made under the seal of an oath, either explicit ("I swear to tell the truth . . .") or implicit, the promise to speak only what I believe to be true. But this oath or promise is, of course, no guarantee against error, lying, perjury, misperception, faulty memory, or any of the other ways a testimony can be untrue, including the possibility that it is a fiction, either in part or through and through. If, on the contrary, all of these possible modes of error could be ruled out (which is not possible), then it would not be what we call testimony but rather of the order of proof, indubitably probative. Consequently, and as Derrida puts it most succinctly in *Demeure: Fiction and Testimony*, "there is no testimony that does not structurally imply in itself the possibility of fiction, simulacra, dissimulation, lie, and perjury—that is to say, the possibility of literature."[6] Finally, then, it is this shared seal of testimony and literature that *puts to the test*

6. Jacques Derrida, *Demeure: Fiction and Testimony*, trans. Elizabeth Rottenberg (Stanford, Calif.: Stanford University Press, 2000), 29.

the essential trait of the nonsecrecy of a death sentence when it requires a witness at its execution.

Before turning to the literary work with which I propose to carry out this test, the short story titled "A Hanging" by George Orwell (1931), I want to anticipate one further question that this text will perhaps allow us to address. As we saw in the previous chapter, Derrida poses the indissociability of a certain modern right to literature and mounting resistance to the death penalty in the guise of a movement for its universal abolition. What remained ambiguous was whether this indissociability also *necessarily* implied that literature would provide a form for that resistance or denunciation rather than just the principle of the right to say anything and everything. To be sure, novels by Hugo, Camus, and Genet (to stay for the moment within Derrida's literary corpus) can be cited as working against the persistence of capital punishment in the era of literature's modernity. But this effect arises, if it does, and as always with a literary work, only through acts of reading and interpretation that cannot simply be programmed in advance by the work itself, still less by an author's intention. No doubt even the unbearable suffering of Hugo's narrator in *The Last Day of a Condemned Man* cannot bypass the interpretation of a reader. This narrator is unnamed because, as Hugo recounts in the 1832 Preface, he wished to "plead the case of any condemned man whatsoever, executed on any day whatsoever, for any crime whatsoever"—in other words, to plead the case for universal abolition, which was the cause to which Hugo remained publicly committed throughout his life.[7] Well, this fictionalized plea depends on an act of reading to which Hugo's novel and its reader can only submit. Indeed, in the dialogued scene Hugo wrote as a preface to his novel when it was initially published in

---

7. Victor Hugo, *Écrits sur la peine de mort* (Arles: Actes Sud, 1979), 10. In this collection of his writings on the death penalty, the first text dates from 1823, when Hugo was twenty-one, and the last from 1885, the year he died.

1829, he predicts an uncomprehending or unsympathetic reception of his work by all but one of the six imaginary interlocutors put on stage.[8] The point is that even a fiction like this one, which wears its abolitionist heart on its sleeve and sacrifices much of the novelist's art to drive its argument home,[9] can be said to work against the death penalty only if its readers undergo the trial by reading—and here reading means identification with the suffering of the other— that every work demands. The space of the work is thereby *both* circumscribed, given once and for all in its inalterable particulars, *and* opened onto the seeming infinity of an interpretive interface where the work is made or allowed or suffered to work in one sense or another. This is, *grosso modo*, the condition under which literary or other works survive as such to be encountered, read, undergone again and again through a strange suspension of precisely the as-suchness of the work as such. Given this condition, it seems unlikely that one could arrive at any satisfying answer to the question: If literature in the modern sense is indissociable from the rise of the struggle for abolition of the death penalty, does this enroll literary works *necessarily* in that struggle?

Despite that, it is a version of this question that George Orwell took up in his weekly "As I Please" column for the *Tribune* on November 3, 1944. Having leafed through a new edition of Anatole France's *Les dieux ont soif*, which is set during the Reign of Terror, Orwell is prompted to reflect: "What a remarkable anthology one could make of pieces of writing describing executions! There must be hundreds of them scattered through literature."[10] After ticking

---

8. See Victor Hugo, *Œuvres complètes*, vol. 19, *Roman II* (Paris: J. Hetzel and A. Quentin, 1881).

9. As Hugo confesses in the 1832 Preface, "So that the argument might be as vast as the cause—and this is why *The Last Day of a Condemned Man* is how it is—[the author] had to cut out everywhere the contingent, the accidental, the relative, the particular, the modifiable, the anecdote, the event, the proper name . . ." (*Écrits sur la peine de mort*, 10; my trans.).

10. http://www.telelib.com/words/authors/O/OrwellGeorge/essay/tribune/index.html.

off selections from Thackeray, Flaubert, Dickens, Byron, Walpole, Zola, London, and Kipling, he remarks:

> The thing that I think very striking is that no one, or no one I can remember, ever writes of an execution with approval. The dominant note is always horror. Society, apparently, cannot get along without capital punishment—for there are some people whom it is simply not safe to leave alive—and yet there is no one, when the pinch comes, who feels it right to kill another human being in cold blood. I watched a man hanged once. There was no question that everybody concerned knew this to be a dreadful, unnatural action. . . . It is probably the fact that capital punishment is accepted as necessary, and yet instinctively felt to be wrong, that gives so many descriptions of executions their tragic atmosphere. They are mostly written by people who have actually watched an execution and feel it to be a terrible and only partly comprehensible experience which they want to record.

Because these are descriptions by witnesses to executions, Orwell is betting that they are "far better written on average than battle pieces" because "battle literature is largely written by people who have never heard a gun go off and think of a battle as a sort of football match in which nobody gets hurt." Thus, according to Orwell, the fact of having "actually watched" or witnessed an execution determines two different but related effects—a higher quality of writing (whatever Orwell means by that) and a reaction of horror, disapproval: "No one, or no one I can remember, ever writes of an execution with approval. The dominant note is always horror." Notice, however, how Orwell presumes that all of this high-quality, horrified writing about capital executions arises out of the contradiction between social expediency and moral revulsion: "Capital punishment is accepted as necessary, and yet instinctively felt to be wrong." What is not envisioned here is any confrontation with that contradiction itself, of the sort, for example, that fuels abolitionist

arguments. A cynic might even wonder if Orwell is content to coun-
tenance the contradiction so long as it stimulates good writing.

To be fair, Orwell is here surveying this literature of witness-to-an-
execution from a considerable distance and dim memory. There is
no pretense of actually rereading any of the merely mentioned texts
to gauge how they negotiate with the horror and to what effect.
These are questions one can pursue, however, in a short narrative
by Orwell himself of the very sort he is compiling here and that
expands his brief reference to a first-hand experience: "I watched
a man hanged once. There was no question that everybody concerned knew this to be a dreadful, unnatural action."

First, however, I want to recall the question from which we set
out and that concerned the shared seal of literature and witnessing.
We're asking, then, about a disturbance or trembling that affects
the defining trait of the death penalty's concept, that is, visibility or
nonsecrecy. For if indeed the death sentence as such requires a witness to its execution, and if the witness's testimony is always sealed
in the ways outlined, then can one ever simply attest to a death
penalty without some remainder of secrecy, or the traces of what
Orwell calls in the passage above an "only partly comprehensible
experience"? Or, in the brief text we are preparing to read, "the
mystery"?

"A Hanging" is one of the first texts published under his pseud-
onym, a short while after Eric Arthur Blair had returned to England
in 1927, ending his career in the colonial police in Burma, which
had lasted five years. Set in Burma (its first line reads, "It was in
Burma, a sodden morning of the rains"),[11] in its main outline the
story is straightforward: Colonial prison officials, including the narrator, gather in a prison yard the morning of the day on which a
man ("He was a Hindu, a puny wisp of a man") is to be hanged. The
narrator recounts how the man is removed from his cell, tied up by

---

11. George Orwell, "A Hanging," in *Facing Unpleasant Facts: Narrative Essays*, ed.
George Packer (New York: Houghton Mifflin Harcourt, 2009), 23; hereafter *AH*.

guards, marched to the gallows, and hanged, after which the officials and guards go back to the yard, relieved that the execution—a
term that is not used—has come off without significant incident.
At the end of the episode, however, all the witnesses to the event,
including the narrator, are laughing—"at what, nobody seemed certain" (*AH*, 28). Now, except for that last note of laughter, the sum-
mary I have just distilled from Orwell's narrative might well have
been made by an official witness to the execution, someone like the
superintendent of police, who in the narrative also records the official time of death. This would be the witness as executor, the one
who gives the order to the hangman, the executioner. It is this same
official witness who verifies that the hanged man is indeed dead,
before noting the time of death: "The superintendent reached out
with his stick and poked the bare body; it oscillated, slightly. '*He's*
all right,' said the superintendent. . . . He glanced at his wrist-watch.
'Eight minutes past eight'" (*AH*, 27).[12]

The witness, however, is not the superintendent but the one
who says "I." A witness is always "I" because only I can bear witness
to what I saw, even if what I saw and witnessed had multiple witnesses, for example, the group of police and prison officials who
watched the man hang that day in Burma. Each of them, of course,
was a witness, but only one is *bearing* witness with this narrative.
I am recalling all this because Orwell's narrator-witness is going to
slide between the singular and plural first persons, between "I" and
"we," as if it were possible to testify collectively or, rather, as if it
were possible to bear witness *for* or *as* the other witnesses. What
happens in these shifts is something of a mystery, as we will see by
following them a little closely through the brief text.

As the narrative opens, "We were waiting outside the condemned
cells" (*AH*, 23). For the next several paragraphs, it is not exactly clear
who this "we" is. There are several persons mentioned—"Six tall

12. On this practice of timekeeping at executions, see Barnaby Norman, "Time of Death:
Derrida/Herzog," *Oxford Literary Review* 35, no. 2 (2013): 205–220.

Indian warders," the prisoner himself—that puny wisp of a man—the superintendent, and "the head jailer, a fat Dravidian in a white drill suit and gold spectacles" named Francis, which is also the only occurrence of a personal proper name in the narrative. And of course, there is the narrator, the one writing "we" and including himself while not yet setting himself apart in any way, unlike the superintendent, who "was standing apart from the rest of us" (*AH*, 23).

Yet the narrator is set apart as, precisely, witness, a witness-narrator (and witnesses are in fact always narrators or potential narrators). Someone is bearing witness in writing—in literature—without yet saying "I." Would that not be the one who signs this eyewitness account as George Orwell? On one level, this seems to be a solid inference, given that about twenty years later, as we already read, the same will sign a newspaper column affirming, "I watched a man hanged once." But all the same, a twist prevents anchoring this attribution of the first person *simply and wholly* in the biographical experience of someone who claims, as Orwell in 1944, to have "actually watched an execution." For it was Eric Arthur Blair, imperial policeman, who "actually watched" but George Orwell who bore witness. What is the difference? Well, I would say it is the difference of *literature*, in other words, an iteration in writing, a *literation* produced when the recollection of an experience requires poetic invention in order to bear witness to an event. But does not testimony always require such invention, since it must be true to an each time *singular* experience or event of witnessing? If only an "I," a singular "I" can bear witness, then this witness has to invent a language or a poetics for its testimony that is not shared with anyone before, precisely, the poetic work begins to exist and to repeat. Yes, exactly.

"A Hanging" is a most interesting example in this regard because the slippage between the singular "I" and the collective "we" of the narration is, in effect, the invention *of* the death penalty, subjective genitive, dictated by its requirement that there be a witness. Orwell's text implies that this witness must be both singular, thus able to narrate and bear witness, *and* collective. We can draw this out further by continuing to follow the turns—and turning asides—of the narration's first person.

"We set out for the gallows," the text continues (*AH*, 24). "We" now includes the party of officials and warders, and of course the prisoner who is being escorted to his hanging. It is thus a sharply fractured collectivity, an abyss opening up there when one of them was condemned (for what crime? by what court? we do not know) to be put to death by the others. Into this fracture comes suddenly the strange eruption of a mongrel dog who dances around the party "wild with glee" before leaping at the prisoner and trying to lick his face. After they manage to control it, this dog is going to accompany the party of men and provide repeated counterpoint to the meaning (or meaninglessness, senselessness) of their acts. This same "large woolly dog, half Airedale, half pariah" is going to whine when the prisoner chants "Ram! Ram! Ram! Ram!" with the noose around his neck while waiting for the trap to open. The dog is also the first to run back behind the gallows after the man has dropped out of sight and "when it got there it stopped short, barked, and then retreated into a corner of the yard, where it stood among the weeds, looking timorously out at us" (*AH*, 27). At us, that is, at we men. This dog, in other words, reminds us to wonder with Derrida, in the first sentence of *The Death Penalty I*, whether "the death penalty is what is proper to man" (*DP I*, 1).

The singular-first-person narrator (and witness) emerges out of this collective humanity once the execution party resumes its march after the interruption, now with dog in tow. The singularized narrator at this point recounts watching the prisoner walk before him ("I watched the bare brown back of the prisoner marching in front of me") and observing the man's steady gait, the smooth working of his muscles, the imprint left by his feet on the gravel, all ordinary physical signs of the other's living being-in-the-world in a body that can leave traces there. But then he sees something that, while it is not in the least out of the ordinary, has the force of an event extraordinary enough to place him before "the mystery, the unspeakable wrongness, of cutting a life short when it is in full tide." Having seen the bound and guarded prisoner step "slightly aside to avoid a puddle on the path," the narrator suspends his account of the inexorable march toward the gallows, stopped in his tracks, as it were, by the other's sidestep. There follows a paragraph in which the narrator confesses to what he had not realized until that moment:

> It is curious, but till that moment I had never realized what it means to destroy a healthy, conscious man. When I saw the prisoner step aside to avoid the puddle, I saw the mystery, the unspeakable wrongness, of cutting a life short when it is in full tide. This man was not dying, he was alive just as we were alive. All of the organs of his body were working—bowels digesting food, skin renewing itself, nails growing, tissues forming—all toiling away in solemn foolery. His nails would still be growing when he stood on the drop, when he was falling through the air with a tenth of a second to live. His eyes saw the yellow gravel and the grey walls, and his brain still remembered, foresaw, reasoned—reasoned even about puddles. He and we were a party of men walking together, seeing, hearing, feeling, understanding the same world; and in two minutes, with a sudden snap, one of us would be gone—one mind less, one world less. (AH, 25)

The tiny event of the sidestep awakens the narrator momentarily out of the collective attitude according to which the man was already (as good as) dead since he had been condemned. This is perhaps why everyone in the party had stood "aghast" when the dog lunges to lick the man, for that gesture calls the living man forth from his own ghost (and the words "aghast" and "ghost" are often associated),[13] thus suspended between the states of not-yet-dead and no-longer-alive. As if the death sentence passed on the man counted already as its execution and the hanging they are there to perform *and* witness

---

13. See the *OED*, s.v. "aghast."

were an empty formality. (But how is it possible for the performer or the executor to be the same as the witness? We will have to come back to this question.) When the narrator observes the man's sidestepping, he in effect steps out of this collective fiction and falls back before the other's reality that stands, walks, and sidesteps *still* on this side of the gallows. And there, standing apart from "us" for the first and only time in the narrative, he "saw the mystery, the unspeakable wrongness" of what "we" were aiming to do in about two minutes.

Except Orwell's narrator pointedly does not connect the dots in this fashion between his singular realization ("till that moment I had never realized") and their collective act. The closest the narrator comes to making the connection is via an abstraction, a generalization: the mystery and wrongness of "cutting off a life when it is in full tide," which at least implies an actor in the action. But when it is *this very* man's coming instant of death that is prefigured, then it is as a passive event, undergone by the condemned man but performed or executed by no one: "when he was falling through the air with a tenth of a second to live"; "and in two minutes, with a sudden snap, one of us would be gone." The mystery, then, concerns the eclipse or disappearance of this "I," who has seen the unspeakable wrongness of his own impending act, into a "we" who is nevertheless going to will and perform that act.

This disappearing act will carry the narrative to the end as the first-person singular dissolves once more into the first-person plural. And the mysteries now begin to proliferate. These signal each time something hidden from the narrator because he either cannot see it or cannot understand it. Twice the condemned man is concealed or partially concealed from sight, first by the flour sack tied over his head, which only muffled but did not silence his "high, re-iterated cry of 'Ram! Ram! Ram! Ram!', not urgent and fearful like a prayer or a cry for help, but steady, rhythmical, almost like the tolling of a bell" (*AH*, 26), and second when the trap opens, where-upon the narrator notes: "The prisoner had vanished, and the rope was twisting on itself" (*AH*, 27). Of course, these disappearances or concealments do not create mysteries so much as they screen the witnesses from the actual face of what they are seeing. But the invisibility they procure prevents all the same the witness from seeing the other die, the instant of his death.

By contrast, the narrator is genuinely mystified by the action or rather the prolonged inaction of the superintendent, who delays giving the order to the hangman while "we stood waiting five yards away." The delay lasts for one long plus one short paragraph:

> The hangman climbed down and stood ready, holding the lever. Minutes seemed to pass. The steady, muffled crying from the prisoner went on and on, "Ram! Ram! Ram!" never faltering for an instant. The superintendent, his head on his chest, was slowly poking the ground with his stick; perhaps he was counting the cries, allowing the prisoner a fixed number—fifty, perhaps, or a hundred. Everyone had changed colour. The Indians had gone grey like bad coffee, and one or two of the bayonets were wavering. We looked at the lashed, hooded man on the drop, and listened to his cries—each cry another second of life; the same thought was in all our minds: oh, kill him quickly, get it over, stop that abominable noise!
>
> Suddenly the superintendent made up his mind. Throwing up his head he made a swift motion with his stick. "Chalo!" he shouted almost fiercely. (*AH*, 26–27)

What heightens the mystery of the superintendent's inscrutable calculation—if he was indeed calculating—is that he was earlier depicted as impatient, precisely, to "get it over." For we first encountered him, in a closely parallel passage, before the party sets off from the prison yard, when, upon hearing eight o'clock strike, he complains about the delay to Francis:

> The superintendent of the jail, who was standing apart from the rest of us, moodily prodding the gravel with his stick, raised his head at the sound. . . . "For God's sake, hurry up, Francis," he said irritably. "The man ought to have been dead by this time. Aren't you ready yet?" (*AH*, 23)

So the narrator is confronted with a mystery within the mystery of the superintendent's suspended impatience: Why did he *delay*? And why did *he*, who was so impatient, delay? Was it perhaps a calculation (counting to fifty or one hundred)? Or was it a wavering of the decision itself as the superintendent sees for himself "the unspeakable wrongness"? Moreover, that the narration remarks one or two "wavering" bayonets in the vicinity of the superintendent's hesitation leaves open the possibility that the text, like dream-work, has operated a displacement from the hidden site onto the visible one, the wavering weapon being above all the one the superintendent hesitated to fire.

That the superintendent's deliberation in his *for intérieur* was an inscrutable mystery is far less surprising, however, than the telepathic transparency that permits the narrator to declare, "the same thought was in all our minds: oh, kill him quickly, get it over, stop that abominable noise!" In the "As I Please" column, Orwell had said something similar to this when he wrote: "I watched a man hanged once. There was no question that everybody concerned knew this to be a dreadful, unnatural action." The similarity shows up in the reduction or abstraction of many—minds, thoughts, convictions—into one and the same. In "A Hanging," this abstraction *articulates* the collective will to put the other to death, to "kill him quickly, get it over, stop that abominable noise!" By "articulates," I mean at least two things: both that it puts into language what had to remain unspoken (because unspeakable) and that it hinges the singular to the plural first person, articulates the thought in "all our minds" with the narrator's own thought—and/or vice versa. This double articulation thus puts us squarely back into that mysterious zone where the singular witness disappears into a collective instance seemingly without remainder, without any residue of what he alone has just seen and witnessed of unspeakable wrongness. In place of this witness, there is the willing agent, performer, executor—executioner, even—of the death penalty: "kill him quickly." Earlier, when I asked if it were possible for the witness to be also the performer or the executor/executioner, it was in anticipation of just this articulating moment in the narrative, when the narrator's singular witness to unspeakable wrongness disappears into the Law, into a willing-the-other-to-death that is collective or shared, "the same thought [that] was in all our minds."

I have suggested that Orwell's text implies a witness to the death penalty who must be both a singular "I" able to bear witness *and* a plural "we," at least two, the executioner and another. For if it is executed without a witness, in secret, then no one can verify what did or did not happen. But the necessary visibility of the death penalty also means that there must always be more than one who *assists* at the execution. Yet, what does it mean to "assist"? In current English, it usually means to help out, give aid, pitch in, lend a hand, have a part in (the subordinate part of someone's "assistant"). The word derives from French *assister* and thus from Latin *assistirer*. Its earliest senses in English, however, which are now obsolete, were close to the still current French sense of *assister*, that is, "to be present at," which is a notion that is more or less indissociable from witnessing. Because a witness is one who was present at an event and is presumed able to testify to what s/he *assisted at*, in the French but no longer English sense. Here is the *OED* on this use:

> *assist, v.*
> 4. a. *intr.* To be present (*at* a ceremony, entertainment, etc.), whether simply as a spectator, or taking part in the proceedings. (In the former case, "to be present *at* without taking part in," now treated as a French idiom.)

The witness assists *at* the execution, but thereby s/he also assists *in* the execution. The two senses of "assist," "assister," have split, side by side and ambiguously, that is, both the sense of "to be present at without taking part in," thus to witness as a neutral *third* party, on the one hand, and the sense of "to be party to the act," assisting in the execution of the act, on the other. A witness is a third party only if s/he is neither executioner nor executed but one who stands apart from the act *assisting at* it, just as the *OED* says, "simply as a spectator" and "without taking part in it." To remain in the position of witness and third party, one must not give *assistance* (a word that in French means simply the audience or those in attendance) by helping to carry out and execute the act of execution. Thus, the one sense of *assistance* cancels out the other. Yet the death penalty, at least as read off of Orwell's exemplary act of literary witness, requires assistance in both senses of the word. This is perhaps the mystery that the narrator has to leave intact: How can the eyewitness who saw what he saw ("When *I saw* the prisoner step aside to avoid the puddle, *I saw* the mystery, the unspeakable wrongness, of cutting a life short when it is in full tide") assist *in* that very act, take part *in* it by giving the order to give the order: "kill him quickly," "'Chalo!'"?

After the hanging, the narrator remains absorbed by the "we" of the party of survivors. His singular first person will surface only once more, very briefly, to remark that, like everyone around him who had witnessed the hanging, he was caught up in a contagious laughter that had spread among them. People were laughing, but "at what, nobody seemed certain." Like the earlier ones, this final mystery of the execution is left hanging even as the narrator suggests that the cause of their laughter is relief. "An enormous relief had come upon us now that the job was done. One felt an impulse to sing, to break into a run, to snigger" (*AH*, 27). Nevertheless, he appears puzzled by his own laughter, or by how loudly he was laughing, when he remarks: "I found that I was laughing quite loudly. Everyone was laughing" (*AH*, 28). This, then, is the point at which the "I" reemerges, but that point is now split or doubled: "I found that I was . . ." To be sure, this phrasing is quite ordinary, but a certain uncanniness clings to it here, as if the narrator had trouble recognizing acts as his own or the sound of his own voice, whether it speaks in unspeakable commands in his head or shouts out loudly in laughter.

These, then, are the mysteries to which the narrator bears witness, beginning with "the mystery, the unspeakable wrongness" he said he saw when he saw the soon-to-be-hanged man sidestep a puddle: "When I saw the prisoner step aside to avoid the puddle, I saw the mystery . . ." Because these are two of the text's very few uses of the verb "to see,"[14] they constitute its most explicit claim to the condition of eyewitness. So a question at this point might be: What does it mean to be eyewitness to a mystery, in other words, to a secret or to something hidden?

In the earliest Greek sense, "mysteries" are, citing again the *OED*, "certain secret religious ceremonies (the most famous being those of Demeter at Eleusis) which were allowed to be witnessed only by the initiated, who were sworn never to disclose their nature." To be sure, the last thing the modern death penalty should resemble is a secret religious ceremony. Yet the eponymous act in "A Hanging" does not altogether avoid comparison with some ancient rite of sacrifice in which the death of the chosen victim procures relief from the community's tensions. Orwell even invites this comparison with the juxtaposition staged in the last two lines of the text: "We all had a drink together, native and European alike, quite amicably. The dead man was a hundred yards away" (*AH*, 28).

If, however, "A Hanging" recounts something like a secret, mysterious rite, then the narrator would be like one of the initiates who has forsworn his oath never to disclose what he has witnessed. It is tempting to cast Orwell in just this role when he forswears service to the colonial police and returns to England planning to write, to become a writer, and when one of the first things he publishes under his new name is this witness account of an execution. We saw how, some fifteen years later in a newspaper column, he conjectured about a link between this witness experience and "good writing." "A Hanging" would be, in this sense, Orwell's full explanation or demonstration of what he means by that. And what it suggests is

---

14. These occurrences are all concentrated in the same paragraph that describes the sidestep. The other three uses are attributed to the condemned man or to everyone "in the party of men walking together, seeing, hearing, feeling, understanding the same world."

that such a witness needs the seal of literary language in order to recount the secret of the death penalty *as* secret. This recounting does not reveal the secret; on the contrary, it never gets to the bottom of the mysteries. But it keeps the secret in the open, in the public domain under the seal of literature and protected free speech in general. Literature here is a seal in at least two senses: it is a seal of secrecy but also a seal of approval, literature as "good writing" and thus, singularly, the seal of Orwell's signature on this little text that protected and preserved it for us to read, for example. And from that protected public space, this literature can always challenge our belief that a death penalty, if there is any, cannot be secret; it must be public before at least one other witness as third party.

Perhaps, then, the only possible witnesses to the impossible secret of a death penalty are poets, known and unknown.

3

IS JUSTICE BURNING?

It is well known that over the course of the last half of the nineteenth and the first half of the twentieth centuries, executions in the West rather abruptly ceased being public affairs. As early as 1868 in the United Kingdom, hangings were no longer carried out in public, and in 1965, capital punishment was largely abolished there.[1] In France, the last public execution by guillotine was in 1939, whereas abolition did not come until 1981. In Italy, the last public execution was in 1947, and capital punishment was abolished there the following year. In West Germany, the last public execution was in 1949, the same year that country abolished the death penalty, while in East Germany executions were never public in that state's short history,

---

1. In Britain, the prevailing argument for removing executions from public view seems to have been that such secrecy would increase the terror of the punishment in the public's imagination. It is a utilitarian argument, although not the usual one of terrifying would-be wrongdoers with the spectacle of terrible punishment. One of those making this other utilitarian argument was John Stuart Mill. See E. S. Burt, "Listening for a Man Swinging: Witnessing in 'The Ballad of Reading Gaol,'" in *Death Sentences: Literature and State Killing*, ed. B. Christ and È. Morisi (Oxford: Legenda, forthcoming).

which abolished the practice entirely in 1987, just three years before reunification.[2] Meanwhile, in the United States, the last public execution, by hanging, took place in 1936 in a state, Kentucky, that is one of the fourteen states to retain the death penalty today (as does both the U.S. federal government and the U.S. military).

Historians of punishment—and there are many—disagree about what compelled parliaments and legislatures to decree this move away from publicity for the ultimate sanction imposed by their penal systems.[3] It has been argued that public executions, rather than deterring crime with the awfulness of these spectacles, attracted and even fomented it, such gatherings acting as magnets for pickpockets, thieves, and public drunkenness. Others argue that it was the boisterous rowdiness of the crowds that offended the class sensibilities of the gentlemen legislators and led them to seek more sheltered conditions in which to carry out executions. According to Michel Foucault, however, this development is but one aspect of the general historical shift in the punishment regime as it became pro-

---

2. With the exception of Tuscany under Leopold II, which abolished capital punishment in 1768, Europe was hardly the leader in worldwide abolition. Earlier were Venezuela (1863), Costa Rica (1877), Panama (1903), Ecuador (1906), Uruguay (1907), and Colombia (1910). In each of these countries, abolition was by constitution. The last legally executed death sentence in South or Central America was in 2000, in Guatemala. https://en.wikipedia.org/wiki/Capital _punishment_by_country.

3. A very partial list would include, among American histories, Stuart Banner, *The Death Penalty: An American History* (Cambridge, Mass.: Harvard University Press, 2002); John Cyril Barton, *Literary Executions: Capital Punishment and American Culture, 1820–1925* (Baltimore, Md.: Johns Hopkins University Press, 2014); William Bowers et al., *Legal Homicide: Death as Punishment in America, 1864–1982* (Boston: Northeastern University Press, 1984); Austin Sarat, *Gruesome Spectacles: Botched Executions and America's Death Penalty* (Stanford, Calif.: Stanford Law Books, 2014); European histories would include Adriano Prosperi, *Delitto e perdono: La pena di morte nell'orizzonte mental dell'Europa cristiana, XIV–XVIII secolo* (Turin: Giulio Einaudi, 2013); William Schabas, *The Abolition of the Death Penalty in International Law* (Cambridge: Cambridge University Press, 1993, 1997); Harry Potter, *Hanging in Judgement: Religion and the Death Penalty in England from the Bloody Code to Abolition* (London: SCM, 1993); Paul Friedland, *Seeing Justice Done: The Age of Spectacular Capital Punishment in France* (Oxford: Oxford University Press, 2012).

gressively, from the end of the eighteenth century onward, a practice of disciplining and reforming individuals rather than instructing the populace, a shift that displaced the display of sovereign power from the public domain to the private, individual one.[4] But contingent and technical factors, instead of grand historical narratives, have also been called upon to explain the move indoors. Eugène Weidmann's beheading by guillotine in France in 1939 was captured clandestinely on film, and images were quickly reprinted the next day in newspapers. Today, the short film sequence has been viewed by millions more on YouTube.[5] Authorities responded by moving executions thereafter within the prison walls.[6] In the United States, the adoption of the electric chair, which was first used in New York in 1890 and quickly became the principal means of executing death sentences in many retentionist states, dictated a move within the prison apparently only for technical reasons. But this technique brought the added benefit of preventing the unwholesome curiosity that could be sparked—forgive the word—by the sort of public spectacles that, in ages past, had been altogether acceptable.

Victor Hugo, the tireless abolitionist, advanced a quite different argument in 1832, more than a century before the last public execution in France. Already he saw signs of the becoming-hidden of the guillotine and its bloody work, which he took as signs of the shame that attached to the continued practice of a barbaric punishment in a supposedly civilized country. Addressing those utilitarians who wanted to believe that executions furnished examples warning of the fate awaiting criminals (the famous deterrent argument), he rid-

---

4. See Michel Foucault, *Discipline and Punish: The Birth of the Prison*, trans. Alan Sheridan (New York: Vintage, 1995).

5. This delayed broadcast of the scene via teletechnology underscores Derrida's point in contradicting Foucault's thesis as concerns the becoming-invisible of punishment; see Chapter 2.

6. The circumstances of this episode are well known, but in her "The Autobiographical Subject and the Death Penalty," *Oxford Literary Review* 35, no. 2 (2013): esp. 169–172 and notes 8–10, E. S. Burt provides precious further insight into it.

icules their reasoning in the face of the recent decision to move the
guillotine from the center of Paris, in the place de la Grève, to what
was then the city's periphery at the Saint Jacques gate:

> But do you seriously believe that you are making an example when
> you so miserably cut the throat of a poor man in the most deserted
> recess of the outer boulevards? At the Grève is one thing, but at
> the Saint Jacques gate? Who passes by there? Who goes there? Who
> knows that you are killing a man there? An example for whom? For
> the trees on the boulevard apparently.
>
> Do you not see, then, that your public executions are being done
> on the sly? Do you not see, then, that you are hiding? That you are
> afraid and ashamed of your work? That you mutter in a ridiculous
> way your *discite justitiam moniti*? That at bottom you are shaken,
> restrained, worried, uncertain of being right, won over by a growing
> doubt, cutting off heads in a routine fashion without really knowing
> what you are doing? . . .
>
> You are leaving the Grève for the Saint Jacques gate, the crowd
> for solitude, daylight for dusk. You no longer do what you do with
> conviction. You are hiding, I tell you![7]

Hugo's diagnosis is plausible: moving the scene of execution out of
view of casual passers-by did indeed betray some shame, the sense
that it was not a fit public spectacle, even as apologists claimed to
believe that the punishment was meant to broadcast the warning
that Hugo phrases in the language of Virgil (*Aeneid*, Book 6), "dis-
cite justitiam moniti": having been warned, learn justice. It is curious, then, how historians of capital punishment have generally
ignored Hugo's insight that the becoming-hidden of executions

7. Victor Hugo, *Écrits sur la peine de mort* (Arles: Actes Sud, 1979), 29–30, my trans.; for
a discussion of this passage, see also Jacques Derrida, *The Death Penalty, Volume I*, ed. Geoffrey Bennington and Thomas Dutoit, trans. Peggy Kamuf (Chicago: University of Chicago Press,
2013), 204–205; hereafter *DP I*.

had something to do with the dawning idea that it was a shameful practice. Its disappearance from the public square would thus have been, according to this insight, but a first step toward its general abolition, an event that Hugo never ceased calling for.

In the West today, however, long after public executions have become all but unthinkable,[8] the walls concealing capital punishment from public view in the one Western and predominantly Christian country that still imposes it, the United States, are no longer just the walls of the prison itself or of the rooms and chambers within it devoted to putting to death the condemned. Class sensibility, fears of crowd reactions, the Foucauldian disciplinary regime, and even, perhaps, Hugo's interpretation of shame can no longer so simply account for the extraordinary measures of secrecy that have grown up around this last surviving remnant of a once common practice in Judeo-Christian societies. Because it constitutes now (and for some time) such a stark exception—American exceptionalism!—not only to patterns found in its own hemisphere but also to trends in Europe, Africa, Asia, and most states of the former Soviet Union, the continued practice of capital punishment in the United States has had to do more than just retreat from public view in order to preserve itself.

So here is an odd idea: The U.S. death penalty is struggling to survive in a largely hostile world, as if it were a living being, an animal, some kind of beast, a human beast perhaps, rather than a cold, deadly cold machine. Odd indeed, yet what if this beastly machine could be seen fighting for its life like any animal when threatened with extinction, its back to the corner? It would have assumed

---

8. I mean unthinkable, of course, in the moral, ethical, or colloquial sense. Public executions remain entirely thinkable and practicable in a number of countries, e.g., Iran, Saudi Arabia, North Korea, and Somalia. And the dissemination by Daesh (ISIS) of its decapitation videos, many of which depict the executions of Europeans and Americans, means that public execution is still actual and at stake in the West as well.

shape, then, as a half-machine, half-human/animal, a singular life form. As singular as the U.S. death penalty up against the hostility of the world.[9]

Meeting resistance and under threat, the U.S. death penalty seeks more and more the protection of secrecy. Many of the retentionist states—Oklahoma, Texas, Florida, Ohio, Missouri, Georgia, etc.— have written laws and protocols that mandate and protect secrecy for a number of the key aspects of their death penalty machinery. As a consequence, membership on execution teams is here or there by law to be kept secret, as are the drugs used in lethal injection as well as the source of these, and any official documents relating to any of these aspects are here or there by law to be kept secret—and thus they are even exempted, by law, from the Freedom of Information Act.[10] Here and there the movement to remove execution from public *view* that began in the nineteenth century is now being extended in a movement to remove it from public *review*. Moreover, this drive to achieve "lethal injection secrecy" leads, as the legal scholar Eric Berger argues, to violations of the Eighth Amendment's "cruel and unusual" clause and thus of the rights, first of all, of the condemned, but as well the rights of a democratic polity to know what its government is really doing. No doubt, this proliferation of secrecy laws around the practice of the U.S. death penalty is in a line of descent from the removal of the gallows or the guillotine

9. "There is far too much secrecy and it's quite indicative [of] the fact that although many countries are giving up the practice, those that retain it nevertheless feel that they have something to hide," said Andrew Gilmour, assistant secretary-general for human rights of the United Nations; "Still Far Too Much Secrecy Surrounding Use of Death Penalty, Says Senior UN Human Rights Official," *UN News Centre*, November 21, 2017, http://www.un.org/apps/news/story.asp?NewsID=58138#.WiWEj0tryis.

10. After listing several sorts of secrecy provisions adopted in various states, the legal analyst Eric Berger continues: "Other states, including Arkansas, Louisiana, Missouri, Oklahoma, South Dakota, Tennessee, and Texas have taken similar routes, passing statutes that officially deem execution procedures secret, sometimes explicitly exempting such materials from state Freedom of Information Act (FOIA) inquiries." Eric Berger, "Lethal Injection Secrecy and Eighth Amendment Due Process," *Boston College Law Review* 55 (2014):1389.

from the public square. In other words, it continues beyond that first modest move of the execution scene from center to periphery, which Hugo already understood as its impulse to hide itself ("You are hiding!" he exclaims). Yet, because it has come manifestly to the *end of the line*, as the last of its kind (which is a Christian-inspired death penalty in what professes to be a democracy), a remnant, remainder, and remains, some break has to happen when it arrives there, at the end, alone. Such a break is signaled when the democratic forms themselves must be violated in order to continue the line, to survive and live on as a death penalty with a future and not just a past.

The secrecy apparently required for the U.S. death penalty's survival, by contradicting and vitiating democratic forms of public review—be they judicial, journalistic, academic, or any other public form—serves as symptom of the autoimmunity that Derrida describes as the impossible condition of democracy (as well as religion).[11] Its mechanisms of defense against threats to its own life having also to attack that life, democracy survives (or not) on the condition of surviving these autoimmune attacks. These take many forms, no doubt, more and more forms, but the form given to autoimmunity by the critical phase now reached by death penalty secrecy in the United States is so manifest, in so many places and in so many ways—laws passed to exempt from the FOIA, for pete's sake!—that one can be relatively certain of not mistaking it for just a passing storm in the autoimmune reactions of the democratic body.

But one should not get too carried away with this odd idea of the U.S. death penalty as a *life form* fighting for survival, for a future. We cannot forget that it is first of all as a *death form* that it will survive, if it does. And as Derrida reminds us, the death penalty does

---

11. See esp. Jacques Derrida, "Faith and Knowledge: The Two Sources of 'Religion' at the Limits of Reason Alone," trans. Samuel Weber, in *Acts of Religion*, ed. Gil Anidjar (New York: Routledge, 2002); and Jacques Derrida, *Rogues: Two Essays on Reason*, trans. Pascale-Anne Brault and Michael Naas (Stanford, Calif.: Stanford University Press, 2005).

and will survive so that "it will always be vain to conclude that the universal abolition of the death penalty, if it comes about one day, means the effective end of any death penalty" (*DP I*, 282). The death penalty survives its death (universal abolition) in, for example, the penalty of life-without-parole, which is to say, in death-in-prison, life without the hope or the future of life *outside*, *without* the prison's walls, which will thus already enclose one's life/death like a coffin. Buried alive, that is the sentence of life-*without*-parole. As the survivor of the death sentence, life-*without*-parole is a death-sentence-*without*-death-sentence. This double "without" is at once performative and privative: performative of the death penalty's survival in this other penalty-without-death-penalty, but also privative of what is called *parole*—but what is that? Parole is the French word meaning, precisely, word, speech, language. To be *sur parole*, on parole, is to be on one's given word, one's promise, one's *parole d'honneur*, and therefore to be in relation to a future because one can promise only on condition of promising to keep the promise into the future. *Parole* as promise is always the promise of some future. Thus, life without parole means life without any future, which is to say death. A life sentence (without possibility of parole) is a death sentence.[12]

When the majority of American public opinion tips (sooner or later) toward abolition of the death penalty, it will also be because the sentence of life has *effectively and affectively* replaced it: effectively, in the juridical equivalence where death sentence = life sentence (without possibility of parole/future), but no less affectively when life is made to equal and thus able to substitute for death.

In the last chapter we considered how literature, in the example

---

12. For an acute analysis of this conversion of the death penalty into life without parole, see Andrew Dilts, "Death Penalty 'Abolition' in Neoliberal Times: The SAFE California Act and the Nexus of Savings and Security," in *Death and Other Penalties*, ed. Geoffrey Adelsberg et al. (New York: Fordham University Press, 2015); see also Charles J. Ogletree Jr. and Austin Sarat, *Life without Parole: America's New Death Penalty?* (New York: NYU Press, 2012).

of Orwell's "A Hanging," tests "the essential trait of the nonsecrecy of a death sentence when it requires a witness at its execution." Put to the test was the affirmation of literature or fiction as the only possible witness to a death penalty because it is impossible. In this chapter, we will see literature's witness raised to another power when the springboard of its fiction is not the death penalty's need for a witness but its drive toward secrecy when it arrives at the end of its line.

The Public Burning, Robert Coover's 1977 novel, restages, as he puts it, "the 1953 Sing Sing executions of the alleged atom spies Julius and Ethel Rosenberg in Times Square as a kind of public exorcism with Uncle Sam as emcee and carny barker."[13] It took Coover more than ten years to see this embryonic idea through to its final published form. By his own account, the idea dawned in 1966–1967 when he was teaching at Bard College. He recalled some years later his sentiment then:

> Although only a little over a decade has passed since this watershed event in twentieth-century American history, my colleagues have largely forgotten the Rosenbergs and my students have never heard of them, though this short-term communal memory loss is probably common to events that become, once recovered from seeming erasure, the iconic or mythic touchstones of a tribe's shared stories. (Log, 84–85)

Coover needed years of research in order to supply the material for one of the novel's principal techniques—collage drawn from contemporary records: trial transcripts, newspaper reports, magazine articles, public speeches, the Rosenbergs' prison correspondence,

---

13. Robert Coover, "*The Public Burning* Log, 1966–77," in *Critique: Studies in Contemporary Fiction* 42, no. 1 (2000): 84. Coover wrote this account of the writing and publishing of the novel in 2000 based on letters and diaries he kept at the time. It is a remarkable text in itself, and I have relied on it throughout this chapter, as signaled hereafter by reference to Log.

congressional debates, biographies of principal characters, FBI files, and so forth. Thus, although unmistakably—and even spectacularly—a fiction, *The Public Burning* is no less certainly documented history retold and narrated without footnotes.

But the necessity for such arduous research (carried out, lest we forget, in an age before Google and the Internet) is not the only reason this novel was in gestation for so long. Another was the choice of Richard Nixon as one of its two main narrators, who alternates with a general third-person narration that itself switches among many tonalities, voices, or "points of view." Nixon himself, the model of the novelistic character, was then still very much an actor on the political stage, especially with his election to the presidency in 1968, reelection in 1972, and resignation of the office in 1974, all of which occurred during the writing of *The Public Burning*. Moreover, never far from these events was the lurching escalation of a war in Vietnam that had been instigated by the so-called domino theory, which had roots in the Red Scare environment of the Rosenbergs' trial and executions in 1953.[14] Thus, Coover's novel composed itself between a specific event in 1953 and the moving target of unfolding events concurrent with the novel's composition. "The book," Coover recorded in 1973 when the Watergate hearings began, "is continually metamorphosing as though invaded by history as a kind of body-snatcher" (Log, 90).

Attending the novel's conception and composition, then, was, on the one hand, body-snatching history and, on the other, the developing, demanding work of fiction to rearticulate present events in a past idiom. This recasting or transposition of one historical moment in terms of the other is related to what Coover calls "the metaphor" of his emerging novel:

---

14. Coover was involved in antiwar protests starting in 1967 at the University of Iowa when he was teaching at its Writers Workshop. His "lyrical documentary" (Log, 85) *On a Confrontation in Iowa City* was filmed during the first antiwar demonstrations there.

The metaphor was still developing then, it was demanding more, and I, far from its manipulator, was slowly sucked into its power. I kept resisting, of course, because I didn't want to be overswept by events since my characters were all living persons mostly from the generation just before ours (the newsmakers of 1953). (Log, 92)

Thus, while on one side, the still unfolding events of history are like body-snatchers, here on the other side, the fiction or metaphor of the Rosenbergs' public, very public burning sucks writing and the writer "into its power": "I, far from its manipulator, was slowly sucked into its power."

The power of the novel's metaphor resides not only in a temporal transposition of two historical moments but also and above all, of course, in a spatial displacement, the entirely fictional transfer of the Rosenbergs' executions from the relative secrecy of Sing Sing's death chamber, where they in fact occurred (on June 19, 1953), to the hyperbolic publicness and publicity of their (fictional) executions in Times Square "with the entire nation in attendance" (Log, 85). The metaphor thus functions in its literal sense, if one may say that: metaphor, from *metapherein*, to carry over, to transfer. The novel exists in and as this metaphoric transfer, which is accomplished narratively over the last three days of the Rosenbergs' lives, when all the judicial, political, journalistic, capitalistic wheels had to turn like clockwork (which is not just a simile here, as we will see) to put them to death. While the narrative of these days and what led up to them follows closely the documented record (one learns a lot about the period and its "newsmakers" from this novel), the most obvious exception is the absurd fiction of the transfer to Times Square.[15] Consequently, as a device, the transfer of the execu-

15. Coover also comments that "history, otherwise kept intact, is disturbed only by my transposition of the actual site of the executions from Sing Sing prison to Times Square, where it is my modest intention to stage a kind of circus, ringmastered by Uncle Sam, with the entire nation in attendance" (Log, 85).

tions, in view of hyperbolic publicity, achieves the same effect for the fiction itself, which stands out absurdly, hyperbolically against its historical background as pure invention, an invention of the impossible.[16]

To carry off this invention and transfer apparently requires an agent or an actor *within* the narrative who will have the power to decide *sovereignly* to execute the Rosenbergs in Times Square and who, despite all the obstacles to such an event—including its outrageous implausibility—can orchestrate it and make it happen. Without such sovereign—necessarily fictional—intervention, the writer is left having to account for what he cannot account for and having to take responsibility for what, as we read, sucked him into its power: the metaphor, the transfer, the executive decision to execute two people, a husband and wife, publicly, as publicly as it is possible to imagine. This other agent or actor, the sovereign decider, within *The Public Burning* is called "Uncle Sam." It is Uncle Sam who produces and stage manages the public burning; he is the supreme executive who decides on the executions by electrocution of Julius and Ethel Rosenberg in Times Square, New York City.

The novel's metaphor, in all its absurdity, has thus to invent a sovereign instance (called Uncle Sam) on which to transfer responsibility for the extravagant transfer it performs. On the first page of the text, in an initial "Prologue" that both sets the stage for the executions to come and gives a condensed account of what has led up to this moment, this transfer is remarked quite unremarkably when

---

16. "So it would be necessary to say that the only possible invention would be the invention of the impossible. But an invention of the impossible is impossible, the other would say. Indeed. But it is the only possible invention: an invention has to declare itself to be the invention of that which did not appear to be possible; otherwise, it only makes explicit a program of possibilities within the economy of the same." Jacques Derrida, "Psyche: Invention of the Other," trans. Catherine Porter, in *Psyche: Inventions of the Other*, ed. Peggy Kamuf and Elizabeth Rottenberg (Stanford, Calif.: Stanford University Press, 2007), 1:44. Derrida's thinking of invention, notably in this essay, provides an alternate way to talk about what has been called (too often perhaps) metafictionality in Coover's work. I will not be able to pursue that idea here.

the third-person narrator relates the circumstances of the (wholly fictional) decision to execute the Rosenbergs in Times Square:

> Then, after the usual series of permissible sophistries, the various delaying moves and light-restoring countermoves, their fate—as the U.S. Supreme Court refuses for the sixth and last time to hear the case, locks its doors, and goes off on holiday—is at last sealed, and *it is determined* to burn them in New York City's Times Square . . .[17]

That "it is determined," left here altogether unanchored in any determined instance of decision, can be attributed only (within the fiction) to the sovereign decider called Uncle Sam. With those three words, the fiction both declares itself and effects the transfer of responsibility for the transfer of the executions.

Uncle Sam is thus the name taken for the other spectacularly manifest fictional—or metaphoric—invention of the novel, a shape-shifting figure incarnated by presidents or would-be presidents like Nixon. Long stretches of the latter's interior monologue, which runs for fifteen chapters, nearly half of the 534-page work, are taken up wondering how this incarnation works, so that he can be ready when his time comes, for he is confident that it will come. When the secret is finally revealed in the novel's "Epilogue," it is the cruelest and most humiliating realization yet in what has been a constant series of humiliations for hopelessly hapless Vice President Nixon. Far from being an incarnation of the spirit of Uncle Sam, it is the latter's monstrous cock that is shoved up Dick's asshole in a violent rape that leaves him writhing with pain and telling himself: "I should have guessed." "I fell back, curled up around my pain. Oh my God, so this was what it was like! I felt like a woman in hard labor, bloated, sewn up, stuffed with some enormous bag of gas I couldn't release. I recalled Hoover's glazed stare, Roosevelt's anguished tics, Ike's silly smile: I should have guessed . . ." (*PB*, 533).

17. Robert Coover, *The Public Burning* (New York: Viking, 1977), 3; emphasis added; hereafter *PB*.

This lusty, violent, and at least at times very corporeal Uncle
Sam is also something like the spirit of the folk. His voluble speech
crosses a very wide range of American idioms, Coover once again
using collage to paste together the character's discourse, which
displays extraordinary invention in the recycling of clichés, half-
remembered quotations, pig Latin, Bible quotations, and on and
on. As Coover confided to an interviewer in 2000, "My idea was
essentially that whenever Uncle Sam spoke, he would be speaking,
literally in the collective voice of the people. It is as though he has
not so much passed through all of those characters, as they have
passed through him, depositing their rhetoric and memories."[18] Just
to take one example (but there would be so many) of this *e pluribus
unum* speech:

> "Well, awright then," thunders Uncle Sam, "straighten up and fry
> right, friends! Go forth to meet the shadowy Future, without fear,
> and with a manly heart on, for they are but anathema maranatha, and
> dirty dogs to boot! Don't fergit that all that has been and is and shall
> be throughout all time are in my hand, so there may be storms in my
> path, but I'll wear a smile, cuz in a little while, my path'll be ro-o-*ses!*
> And so, trustin' in Him who can go with me, and remain with you,
> and be everywhere for good and anon, let us remember the *Maine,*
> cock a snook, cover the embers and put out the light—toil comes
> with the morning, and broil with the night! Hoo hah! God bless you
> all!" (*PB,* 109)

The metaphor that sucks the writer into its power is operating
also at this fine-grained level where, after all, writing has to happen. It is there too, first of all and finally, the writer has to do what
Coover calls surrendering to the metaphor. In his "*Public Burning
Log: 1966–1977,*" he records this surrender as a condition of the
condition of writer: "I may be writing this book the rest of my life,

---

18. "As Guilty as the Rest of Them: An Interview with Robert Coover," *Critique: Studies in
Contemporary Fiction* 42, no. 1 (2000): 119.

which would be manifestly crazy, even I can see that. But here's the problem: if I cured myself of this somehow, if I could just live with a metaphor instead of surrendering to it, I couldn't write. I'd have to quit" (Log, 92).

That was Coover's sentiment in August 1974, just as he began to see the end of his long tunnel through the writing of *The Public Burning*. Still to come, however, were all the episodes, lasting almost two years, with the legal departments of successive publishers (Dutton, Knopf, Simon & Schuster, Harper, and finally Viking), which were all very anxious about liabilities entailed by the extravagant license taken in the book with living persons—Nixon and family foremost, but the list of potential plaintiffs was long given Coover's faithful adherence to historical record. The publishers' lawyers made myriad proposals for revision in view of lowering risk; few of these were reasonable, and many were simply risible, such as the suggestion that Coover use a different narrator instead of Richard Nixon, someone already dead such as, for instance, Eleanor Roosevelt (Log, 98). Very interesting in all of this wrangling is what is conveyed to Coover one day in 1976 by an editor at Knopf who reports the remarks of Benno Schmidt, then dean of Columbia University's law school, brought in as a legal consultant by the publisher. According to Schmidt, "there is not any jurisprudence in this area, no case of a real person having been made a protagonist in a work of fiction having come before the courts. Nor has any court indicated if the First Amendment protects fantasy" (Log, 98–99). While it would seem to be untrue today, forty years later, that no court has ruled on First Amendment protection of fantasy,[19] Schmidt's first observation seems still valid, to wit, that no court has

---

19. See, for example, *United States v. Valle*, in which a 2014 district court decision threw out the conviction of a man for violent fantasies on an Internet chat room, or *Ashcroft v. Free Speech Coalition* (2002), a Supreme Court decision that struck down a law banning virtual child pornography. But fantasy concerning living persons in fictional literature like *The Public Burning* would appear to remain untested by the courts.

recognized arguments that literary fiction does not have the right
to appropriate living persons to its fantasies. And what this points
up is how far *The Public Burning* went not just in making a few
publishers' lawyers nervous but in shaking up basic presumptions
about the laws of literature. Above all, it confirms that literature's
right to say anything—about the living and the dead, the fantasized
and the real—cannot be abrogated without undermining a fundamental trait of democracy.[20]

"No democracy without literature; no literature without democracy": This is perhaps the lesson of *The Public Burning* not only
through its trials with the law and with lawyers but also through the
literary, fictional act that it is and that it narrates in several voices. It
is this question of the narrative's voice or voices that links up with
the question of democracy, where voices are supposed to count and
be counted. But how to count the voices in *The Public Burning*? I
have already mentioned that Uncle Sam speaks "literally in the collective voice of the people." He is thus constructed, literally,[21] as
the fiction of "the people" speaking with one voice. Moreover, he
is not the only site at which from *pluribus* one gets *unum*. Another
is TIME, personified as the National Poet Laureate, whose biography is recounted in Chapter 18, where he is also shown wandering
through the crowd in Times Square "collecting images, experiment-
ing with various forms and meters, searching for the metaphoric
frame by which to contain and re-create tonight's main event" (*PB*,

20. This categorical assertion is not contradicted or even limited by the fact that would-be
democracies have practiced, or continue to practice, censorship in many forms. On the contrary, such shortcomings underscore the necessity of thinking democracy not as a presence
but always in the form of the "to-come," as democracy-to-come. On this necessity, see Derrida,
Rogues.

21. That is, literally cut and pasted. In his interview with Larry McCaffery for the special issue of *Critique* devoted to *The Public Burning*, Coover describes how he "collected thousands
of one-liners and typed them all out with carbon copies, cut them up and spread them around
on the tables and floor, and played with them in the context of the events and Cold War fever
of June 1953" ("As Guilty as the Rest of Them," 119).

319–320). As the people's poet he lets them know all they need to know through his "art of subordinating facts to the imagination, of giving them shape and visibility, keeping them *personal*" (PB, 320). TIME is (or are[22]) the no-one poet of the personal everyone. He does not so much collect the people's voices like Uncle Sam as convert them into popular lyrics—and several passages from TIME articles are indeed set as verse in the novel's pages.[23] There is also the one the novel calls "the Spirit of History," that is, the *New York Times*, which is another force for countering dispersion and difference by collecting all and sundry in one place. It is depicted as a kind of temple of worship from which issue tablets that have the power to connect the totally unconnected, to make continuity out of the discontinuous and knit the world of its "worshipers" into one.[24]

Even though, as Coover could affirm some years later, "the much-feared legal assault on the book did not happen,"[25] *The Public Burning* had still been successively refused by several major publishing houses, only to be allowed to go out of print two years after it finally did appear. It remained so for twenty years until it was reissued by Grove-Atlantic in 1998.

Before going any further with *The Public Burning*, I should say something about the selective, fragmentary, and above all slanted reading of it proposed here. The slant is toward the central question of the present book, which is asking how literature resists the death penalty or at least exposes it to its undoing. In a certain sense, however, Coover's novel is not at all concerned with THE death penalty

22. This noun is occasionally treated as a plural, for example, "TIME say . . ." (PB, 43).

23. See, for example, PB, 43–44.

24. This depiction is essentially congruent with Benedict Anderson's argument that daily newspapers have been a key tool in binding together the imagined communities of nationalism; see Benedict Anderson, *Imagined Communities: Reflections on the Origins and Spread of Nationalism* (London: Verso, 1983; 2nd ed. 1991; 3rd ed. 2006).

25. "Robert Coover on *The Public Burning*," http://www.flashpointmag.com/cooverpub burn.htm.

as such but rather with the Rosenbergs' executions and with that specific injustice—for, whether or not they were actually innocent or guilty as charged, it was an injustice and a gross one.[26] Yet, in another sense, the novel is entirely taken up with depicting, through its metaphoric lens, the forces that dictate and sustain a death penalty regime, which includes the public that is determined by such a regime. While these depictions are richly informed in the novel by the specific detail of the Rosenbergs' case, they can also be generalized through the logic of example. They would thus also be depictions, via the example, of the American death penalty in general.

This logic of example has largely guided my selective "reading" of the novel—less a reading than a sampling. For *The Public Burning* is a huge, unencompassable tapestry. Its tirelessly inventive language—meshing phrases, verses, rhymes, songs, lyrics, chants, quotations, movie scripts, trial transcripts, and what have you—can take your breath away as you try to take it in. Obviously I do not pretend to do justice to the scope of the novel's achievement.[27] Moreover, the novel invokes a patterned understanding of meanings that I mostly neglect. There is, above all, the apocalyptic theme, which Coover began to explore and exploit in his previous lengthy novel, *The Origin of the Brunists* (1966), along with its connection to the formation of religions and cults.[28] *The Public Burning* bids, among so many other things, to be a full-blown account of the American civil religion that liberally mixes invocations of Christianity with

26. For a cogent review of the arguments that have persisted on both sides, see Robert Wilbur's essay "The True Crime of the Rosenberg Execution," http://www.truth-out.org/news/item/1537:the-true-crime-of-the-rosenberg-execution.

27. Coover recounts that one of the first readers of the novel in manuscript, Jackson Cope (later the author of *Robert Coover's Fictions* [Baltimore, Md.: Johns Hopkins University Press, 1986]), ecstatically told him he had "finally sunk *Moby Dick.*" Coover comments: "A bit over the top, but at least I'm reassured it's not utter folly" (Log, 98).

28. Robert Coover, *The Origin of the Brunists* (New York: G. P. Putnam's Sons, 1966). In 2014, Coover published a 1,005-page sequel to this novel: *The Brunist Day of Wrath* (Ann Arbor: Dzanc, 2014). Dzanc Books also reissued *The Origin of the Brunists* in 2015.

politics—its political theology and theopolitical brand of sovereignty—and that stages the public spectacle of the executions as a
sacrificial rite for the security of the nation but also as a reinvigora-
tion of the community of believers.[29] The sociology of religion, as
propounded by Durkheim and Weber, can be seen to help shape
the novel's plot and to direct to an important extent the conversion
of its central metaphor—the public burning—into narrative. Even
its organization into chapters that alternate between a general third-
person narration and Richard Nixon's silent first-person confessions
and cogitations could be aligned with Durkheim's reliance on the
principle of mutual dependence between society and individual. All
of this is certainly of interest and pertinent for my own main question about the exceptional persistence of the death penalty in the
same America that Coover portrays through its civil religion. I have
tried to keep it in view even as I slant off in other directions.

"The whole book is meant to have the feel of a ticking clock; it's a
countdown to the moment that the Rosenbergs are going to die."[30]
The novel, then, would make or let its readers feel time as a relation to death calculated to arrive at a certain moment by the clock.
Victor Hugo would have recognized Coover's intention here. His
novel *The Last Day of a Condemned Man* is likewise structured by
a clock ticking down toward a man's death.[31] For Hugo the countdown structure carries the abolitionist aim of his novel, which was
meant to touch the humanity of those who pass death sentences, to

29. For an extended account of the novel in these terms, see Robert Detweiler, *Uncivil
Rites: American Fiction, Religion, and the Public Sphere* (Urbana: University of Illinois Press,
1996).
   30. "As Guilty as the Rest of Them," 121.
   31. Hugo describes his own experience of the countdown when the painful idea of an
imminent execution filled his mind and "explained to him hour by hour the last sufferings of
the miserable one who was dying—now he is confessing, now his hair is being cut, now his
hands are being tied." He could not breathe until four o'clock, "once the *ponens caput expi-
ravit* [was] cried out by the sinister voice of the clock." Hugo, *Écrits sur la peine de mort*, 11.

make the heart of the magistrate bleed.[32] Coover's novel inherits, even if unintentionally, from this abolitionist tradition, but its "feel of a ticking clock" has little of the grim pathos that Hugo relied on;[33] instead, it stages a circus, a carnival, a ceremonial gathering turned into gross slapstick. Perhaps like the rowdy spectators at executions when these were still (really) public, the crowd in Times Square is taken hold of by something atavistic, tribal, primitive. Pressed together "elbow to elbow, and belly to butt," the crowd of people "watch the clocks tick away the last of the Rosenbergs' time on earth" (PB, 401). As the clocks tick down, the crowd writhes closer to the full-out orgy that finally breaks out minutes before the countdown was calculated to end. Thus, the countdown clocks drive a strong sexual current running through the narrative, exciting the crowd in Times Square with a "strange randy unease they've been feeling all day, ever since waking this morning in their several states of suspended excitation" (PB, 92). And not just the nameless masses but all the land's powerful men and women—and names are named[34]—are similarly aroused on the day the final countdown

---

32. "The present author," reports Hugo, will be "happy if, without any instrument other than his thought, he has dug deep enough beneath the œs triplex to cause the heart of the magistrate to bleed! . . . happy if, by dint of drilling down into the judge, he has occasionally succeeded in finding again the man!" Écrits sur la peine de mort, 10.

33. But it certainly does not avoid this pathos altogether. See in particular the beginning of Chapter 16, where, to the TV announcement of the vacated stay by the Supreme Court and Eisenhower's refusal of clemency, a ten-year old boy in the Bach household in Toms River, New Jersey, murmurs in response, "My Mommy and Daddy," as he realizes "That was their last chance . . . trying to picture this new finality" and wonders "why is [the world] killing his Mom and Dad like this" (PB, 277–278). This appears to be a trace in the novel of an earlier version before Coover negotiated a settlement with Michael and Robert Meeropol (nés Rosenberg) and their lawyer; see Log, 107, 109.

34. The novel names names a lot throughout, in particular the names of those who named names before the House Un-American Activities Committee. In Chapter 10, "Pilgrimage to The New York Times," the act of public naming is characterized thus: "In the old days, before The New York Times, if you wished to destroy a man, you inscribed his name on a pot and smashed it. Or stuck a clay image with a pin. Now you attach his name to a sin and print it. Such an act is beyond mere insult or information, it is a magical disturbance of History" (PB, 194).

begins: "all awakened this morning with prodigious erections and enflamed crevices" (*PB*, 163).

This mounting sexual feeling is another face of the novel's central conceit or metaphor of the *public burning*—noun plus adjective, a public *that is* burning and making it (in) public. This other burning entails that something reserved for privacy—one's privates, they are called—be hung out in public for anyone nearby to grab onto. An orgiastic delirium of excitement and terror overcomes the crowd when Uncle Sam, who is managing the show for Coover, douses the lights and plunges everything into darkness. This prompts the general narrator to observe:

> It is astounding to consider how many orifices, large and small, and how many complementary protuberances, soft and rigid, the human body possesses, all the more so when that number is raised to the nth power by jamming thousands of such bodies several layers deep into a confined space and letting everything hang out! (*PB*, 492)

Among the compacted layers of orifices and protuberances, this burning public display, "letting everything hang out" and in the "seizure of imminent orgasm" (*PB*, 492), allegorically or metaphorically enacts the fusion of the community of the faithful brought together through sexual excitement and terror. The terror and its attendant arousal dissipate only once Uncle Sam brings the lights back up and asks the crowd for "a mite less indecent exposure!" (*PB*, 495).

In its insistence on the link between one public burning and the other, between public execution and indecent exposure,[35] the novel has perhaps something to say today about the secrecy that protects death penalty practices in the United States. It could prompt one to ask, for example: What if the drive to secrecy were not just a symptom of the remains and the last throes in the life of the U.S. death penalty, as I suggested above, but an essential trait of the

---

35. Dr. Alfred Kinsey, we learn, has been "invited here tonight to pursue his celebrated studies into the effects of electrocution upon the erogenous zones" (*PB*, 357).

modern death penalty? By "modern death penalty," I mean a post-Enlightenment practice of capital punishment, the one that coexists with abolitionist discourse as initiated in the eighteenth century in Europe. In this modern form, as continued up to its last remainder and avatar today in the United States, the death penalty has perhaps also been driven by the urge to indecent exposure, which has to call up the contrary drive to keep hidden what should not be exposed. This suggestion would align with Hugo's perception of the shame that had begun to attach to capital punishment in the early nineteenth century and that would have initiated the historical retreat of execution scenes, in the age of the modern death penalty, from the public square. Because Coover's novel reverses this historical movement by dragging the scene out of the prison and into the center of a public spectacle, it also drags into the open the shamelessness of the spectators that such a reversal has to suppose. The scene has to be obscene.

Recall that all this obscene arousal is tied to a clock ticking down. As you might expect, there are clocks being glanced at everywhere in the novel. Calculations of time are constantly being made. When the narrative opens, Justice William O. Douglas (to whom the novel is dedicated) has just granted a stay, which stops the countdown and will delay the execution initially scheduled for the next day, Thursday, June 18, 1953. The suspension lasts until Friday at noon (High Noon, which is the title, we learn, of President Eisenhower's—Ike's—favorite movie, in a chapter of the same name), after the full Supreme Court, hurriedly called back into session from their summer recess, has vacated the stay and the president has refused a final appeal of clemency before announcing that the execution will take place eight hours later. Because of the day's delay, which postpones it from a Thursday to a Friday, the execution must be over before sundown and the beginning of shabbat, out of respect for the Rosenbergs' Jewish community.[36] On Friday, June 19,

---

36. Thus another law, Jewish law, takes over the calculations of sovereign U.S. (Uncle Sam's) law. Even though its authority forces only a delay, a stay rather than an interruption, this

1953, sunset was at 8:31 Eastern Daylight Time. The sabbath would have begun at 8:13.[37] Julius was executed at 8:01, but Ethel was not pronounced dead until 8:16, her death by electrocution having required two more than the customary three jolts.

Coover's novel respects all these recorded details, if indeed one can call massive doses of electricity applied with lethal intention a detail. The calculation of clock time is thus a preoccupation throughout the novel. But time or the times are also constantly being invoked as proper names, titles, or toponyms. Times Square (not a square, just a busy intersection) takes its name from One Times Square, a building that in turn takes its name from the *New York Times*, which at the start of the last century was briefly headquartered there. Beginning in 1908 and every year since, One Times Square has counted down to the new year with the downward movement of a ball, such a representation of time passing being reason enough apparently for celebration. Up above the square named for the *Times*, a four-faced clock atop the thirty-three stories of the Paramount Building is visible from the cardinal points of the compass, thus encompassing in its measure all who can see it. Below, in another dimension, we have already glimpsed the Poet Laureate, looking for the truth that only TIME can tell.

This countdown that measures out the remainder of a life, that fixes time of death in an advance calculation, is an essential trait of what Derrida identifies as the phantasm that sustains and is sustained by the death penalty. It is a phantasm of mastery over the time of life, represented as the time remaining in a countdown, which is known in advance. "This knowledge," Derrida writes, "this mastery over the time of life and death, this mastering and calculating knowledge of the time of life of the subject is presupposed—note that I say presupposed—alleged, presumed in the very concept of the death penalty" (*DP I*, 220). The death penalty, in other words,

---

instance of another law shows up a limit on the law's sovereignty, on its principle of undivided, unshared, unlimited authority.

37. These precise calculations are made on *PB*, 425.

is a concept-tool for counting down to the end of life with advance knowledge of time and thus a machine for calculating incalculable finitude. And because it presumes a knowledge in which objective time (clock time) coincides with the subjective time of the one condemned to death, its specific and greatest cruelty, Derrida avers, is inflicted as this experience of time.[38] Further on in the seminar, he underscores clearly the phantasmatic condition of this knowledge and this mastery but also the seductive fascination it exerts:

> Whence the seduction that it can exert over fascinated subjects. . . .
> Fascinated by the power and by the calculation, fascinated by the
> end of finitude, in sum, by the end of this anxiety before the future
> that the calculating machine procures. The calculating decision,
> by putting an end to life, seems, paradoxically, to put an end to
> finitude; it affirms its power over time; it masters the future; it
> protects against the irruption of the other. In any case, it *seems* to do
> that, I say; it only seems to do that, for this calculation, this mastery,
> this decidability, remain phantasms. It would no doubt be possible to
> show that this is even the origin of phantasm in general. (*DP I*, 258)

Derrida goes on to comment that the phantasm of putting an end to finitude is no doubt invincible, which explains the "fascination exerted by the real phenomena of death penalty and execution." I quote another long passage with the excuse that it will send us back to Coover's novel with a different eye for the spectacle it stages:

---

38. Richard Nixon's character in *The Public Burning* seems to understand right away this cruelty of time when, upon being told by the Sing Sing prison Warden that electrocution or "'electrolethe as we used to call it'" is painless and instantaneous ("'the current melts the brain so fast that the nervous system probably doesn't even have time to register any pain'"), he reflects to himself: "It's not the shock itself that hurts, I thought, goddamn it, my own brain tingling, it's the anticipation" (*PB*, 412). For all the ways in which he is manifestly the bumbling clown of this circus, Nixon's character is no less the principal node of a sympathetic connection to the Rosenbergs. It leads him to formulate thoughts about death and the death penalty that can be arresting in their insight, for example: "I was thinking: the old legends about Death were closer to the truth than the ones we had now—it was a substantial reality, a kind of person, an active intervention in the endless process of life" (*PB*, 413).

The fascination exerted by the real phenomena of death penalty and execution, this fascination of which we could give so many examples, has to do with its effect of truth or of acting out [*passage à l'acte*]: we then see it as actually staged; we project it as one projects a film or as one projects a project; we see in projection actually enacted what we are dreaming of all the time—what we are dreaming of, that is, what in a certain way we desire, namely, to give ourselves death and to infinitize ourselves by giving ourselves death in a calculable, calculated, decidable fashion; and when I say "we," this means that in this dream we occupy, simultaneously or successively, all the positions, those of a judge, of judges, of the jury, of the executioner or the assistants, of the one condemned to death, of course, and the position of one's nearest and dearest, loved or hated, and that of the voyeuristic spectators who we are more than ever. (*DP I*, 258)

Note that these fascinatingly real phenomena are no less taking place in a kind of theater: What we see is staged (*mise en scène*); one projects the scene like a film; there are actors and spectators.[39] The real phenomena have the effect of what Derrida calls a *passage à l'acte*, acting out in an at least quasi psychoanalytic sense, which places the scene also in a psychic theater where the death penalty arouses or tempts a desire.[40] This psychic theater of the death penalty is most clearly evoked in the assertion that "we see in projection

---

39. This theatrical or cinematic dimension of executions is repeatedly underscored by Derrida in *DP I*. As mentioned in Chapter 2, it is this "technical, tele-technical, or even tele-visual complication of seeing" (*DP I*, 43) that he cites when contesting Foucault's thesis of the disappearance of "the great spectacle of physical punishment" (Foucault, *Discipline and Punish*, 14).

40. In their *Vocabulaire de la psychanalyse* (Paris: PUF, 1967), J. Laplanche and J.-B. Pontalis prefer the phrase "mise en acte" to translate Freud's use of *agieren*, which is rendered as "acting out" in English. Laplanche and Pontalis's short definition is: "According to Freud, act or deed [*fait*] with which the subject, under the power of his/her unconscious desires and fantasms, lives them in the present with a feeling of actuality that is all the stronger because s/he misrecognizes their origin and repetitive nature" (240; my trans.). Because *passage à l'acte* is a common idiom in French, the analysts forge the phrase "mise en acte" so as to give it a limited clinical sense. (My thanks to Elizabeth Rottenberg for her help with psychoanalytic vocabulary.)

actually enacted [*nous voyons en projection s'effectuer en acte*] what we are dreaming of all the time." As if in a movie theater, "we see in projection," but the figure of projection can likewise have a psychoanalytic value or valence here. What we see we have also projected, exteriorized, literally "thrown before" and in front of our own eyes.[41]

The Public Burning puts this scene on stage, which is to say it stages the staging, projects the projections, and doubles the already doubled space of the *passages à l'acte*. We have seen how the crowd arrives at Times Square on an erotic tide, their most basic sexual repressions having been given the day off. The last chapter before the epilogue, which is the longest of the twenty-eight, picks up right after Uncle Sam has plunged everything into darkness, setting off a panic fear that the Phantom—that is, the archenemy, Communism—has triumphed before the lights come back up. Now comes the final act and acting out. As in all the chapters narrated in the third person, the perspective is highly mobile, pulling back for the most general view of the whole crowd of spectators, then zooming in to pick out the different actors. Fictionally convened at the same time and place of execution are all those figures that Derrida lists as brought together in the dream of capital punishment in which each dreamer occupies plural positions. In the drama about to unfold its final act, the narration passes through these various positions one after the other: from judges to prosecutors to the jury to the president who did not grant clemency, then back to the anonymous, voyeuristic spectators.

By the time the final actors come on stage—the executioner and assistants, the rabbi and Julius Rosenberg—"a respectful hush has fallen over Times Square: *they are about to see a man die . . .*" (*PB*, 506; emphasis added). From behind a screen, the Executioner pulls a switch.

---

41. In a 2001 interview in *Cahiers du cinéma*, Derrida insists on this two-way projection as the "mechanism of cinema"; see Jacques Derrida, "Cinema and Its Ghosts," trans. Peggy Kamuf, *Discourse* 37, nos. 1/2 (Winter/Spring 2015).

Julius Rosenberg's body is straining suddenly against the straps as though trying to burst from the chair. Air hisses from his lungs. His neck thickens as though swallowing something whole. The leather straps creak and there is a staticky crackling whine in the Square reminiscent of the classic mad-doctor movies—only more close up. The loose clothes flutter and the limbs shake. Greasy yellow-grey smoke plumes from the top of his head like a cast-out devil. Then, abruptly the whine stops. The body falls back into the chair, limp as a rag. There is a deathly breath-held silence in Times Square.[42] Before it can be broken, the Executioner methodically pulls a switch a second time and again the body leaps from its seat to heave and labor against its shackles. By the time the third charge is delivered, there are still a lot of gaping mouths and bulging eyeballs out front . . . but on the whole, the worst is past: *they've seen it now and know what to expect*. (*PB*, 509–510; emphasis added)

In the passage from being "about to see a man die" to having "seen it now," a knowledge is produced or, rather, a presumed knowledge, in that they now "know what to expect." The given context here of a double execution works to absorb the otherwise striking ambiguity of this knowledge and this expectation. That is, in this context we understand that they now presume to know what to expect when Ethel Rosenberg will be executed a few minutes after her husband. The idea is that one execution must be just the same as any other, that they've seen it once, so now they know it and know what to

---

42. This silence is also that of a theater. The word "silence" is initially singled out in the novel on a sign tacked up over the door by which the Rosenbergs enter onto the execution stage. The same word is also on a sign over an exit door on the stage of the last "Intermezzo" between the third and fourth parts of the book, which is subtitled: "A Last-Act Sing Sing Opera by Julius and Ethel Rosenberg." This theatrical piece ends when Julius turns to the audience and "with sudden intensity" asks "WHAT WILL BE THE RESPONSE OF AMERICA TO ALL THIS?" In response, the last stage direction is: "A lone spotlight lingers momentarily on this sign, which reads: SILENCE" (*PB*, 394). As Nixon discovers when he goes there, the sign also hangs over the door leading to the Death Cells at Sing Sing. With this one-word sign, then, the novel connects the space of the theater and the execution chamber or stage, as if it were the very name of the portal connecting them. But "silence" also names the Rosenbergs' "crime," that is, their refusal to name names and to confess.

expect the next time they see a man—or a woman—executed in this manner. They thus presume that death can be calculated, made knowable, predictable, foreseeable as an iterable event, for now "they know what to expect."

But if one lets that phrase dangle free of this context for a moment, then its phantasmatic charge can register. For indeed, can anyone ever *know*, fully know what to expect in the way of death? Is not such foreknowledge and mastery of death the phantasm of the death penalty, which may be the origin of all other phantasms? As we will see, even in the context announced again by this final chapter's title, which is "The Burning of Julius and Ethel Rosenberg," even in this context of an apparent repetition, first one then the other, there will have been no knowing what to expect, no knowledge at all therefore. No doubt the retrospective provided by this interruption of knowledge, repetition, and expectation shows up the error of believing one knew what to expect as death, the other's and, by projection, one's own, "my" own. This is the great phantasm produced by the desire that Derrida describes as the desire to give oneself one's own death as a calculable, calculated, known, *expected* event. Finitude, which means above all that I can never "know what to expect," is canceled, suspended, ended—*finie la finitude*—in-finitized, *as it were*. This "as it were" is the remains and trace of the phantasm, which the fiction retrieves and registers for us to read.

When Ethel Rosenberg comes on stage, her person, carriage, and expression announce that something unexpected is happening. Her very presence declares "that, unlike Shaw's Saint Joan, she will not be burned offstage—indeed, even had this been the plan, she would not have allowed it" (*PB*, 512). (Notice we are still in a theater, but in the theater of a death penalty where there is no offstage.)[43] The

43. Everything in *The Public Burning* is always happening in some theater or with reference to theatrical performance, plays, acting, etc. (see note 42). Coover has said that he first began writing what became the novel as "street theater or commedia dell'arte" to be performed in Times Square (Log, 84).

narrator observes the effect on the crowd. Some of them, "feeling they've seen all there is to see the first time around," have become restless, "but Ethel's entrance has changed all that" (*PB*, 512–513). Here is how the narrator explains what has changed for them:

> Julius shared his terror with them all, and so they were able to sympathize with him, get inside and *suffer what he suffered, then survive*—but Ethel is insisting on being herself, forcing them to think about something or someone other than themselves, which is both disquieting and exciting. (*PB*, 513; emphasis added).

The difference, then, is a matter of survival. As Julius, the spectators could both suffer death and survive it, the ultimate phantasmatic pleasure. But Ethel insists on being herself, rather than the vehicle of their survival. Above all she looks at them: "She gazes around the set and out into Times Square with a kind of fierce delight, enjoying what she sees, meeting each of her accusers with a bold steady stare, smiling at the people beyond, daring them all to watch and listen. . . ." (*PB*, 513). This ellipsis in the text is followed by a verse from Psalm 31, as intoned by the rabbi who accompanied the condemned woman: "'For I have heard the slander of many,' reads the rabbi, 'fear was on every side: while they took counsel together against me, they devised to take away my life!'" (*PB*, 513).[44] David's words are here put in the mouth of the silent woman as she meets her accusers' eyes. Her "bold steady stare" does not flinch even as she is strapped in the chair and "the black leather hood comes down, covering her face" (*PB*, 515).

---

44. In *The Book of Daniel*, which was a fiction also based on the Rosenberg executions and published a few years before *The Public Burning*, E. L. Doctorow portrays quite a different interplay with the rabbi. The narrator here is the son of the condemned woman: "Then my mother's eyes lighted on the prison rabbi [among the witnesses to her execution]. It was the same man whose ministrations she had refused for the last forty-eight hours. 'I will not have him here,' she said. The rabbi in his tallis and yarmulke walked toward the door. Before he was gone my mother called after him: 'Let my son be bar mitzvahed today. Let our death be his bar mitzvah.'" E. L. Doctorow, *The Book of Daniel* (New York: Random House, 1971), 297–298.

The difference is a matter of survival in another wholly unexpected manner when Ethel survives—very briefly—the law's best calculation for putting her to death. The execution protocol calls for three discharges of electricity into the body to ensure that death ensues. After the third shock, Ethel certainly looks dead and everyone assumes the show is over, the deed is done, the sentence has been executed, when the doctor who must officially pronounce death and record the time exclaims, "*This woman . . . is still alive!*" (*PB*, 516). There is no protocol for the circumstance; the law has not calculated what to expect to do next; general confusion results. The Executioner is "scratching his head in stupid bewilderment" and "seems confused, indecisive"; the Warden has "lost the initiative"; doctors are aimless because "thrown into this ad lib situation," but once again Uncle Sam rouses the people from their stupor and sounds a charge on the lethal mechanism, to which responds a long list of volunteers ("led by Dick Nixon, followed by Joe McCarthy, Herb Brownell, Bill Knowland, Lyndon Johnson, Foster Dulles and Allen, Engline Charlie, and Estes Kefauver, virtually the entire VIP section" [*PB*, 516–517]) to throw the switch again. They fall over one another to reach it first, and they collectively pull on it "with such force they snap the thing clean off!" (*PB*, 517).

With its grotesque satire, this scene lays bare a *passage à l'acte* stripped of the cover of law and the mediation of calculation. All that is left is a surplus or excess of force, which is exerted in a collective compulsion (a redundancy when one recalls a little etymology here: *com-pellere*, to drive together). Ethel's still beating heart has compelled the compulsion to show itself as bare *passage à l'acte.*[45] It thus defies the law's sentence and the calculation of time in a countdown to execution. Recall that the countdown was set to end before the beginning of shabbat at 8:13 p.m. But the *passage à*

---

45. In his *Gruesome Spectacles (195)*, Austin Sarat includes Ethel Rosenberg's electrocution in the appendixed list of 276 botched executions in the United States between 1890 and 2010.

l'acte will ignore this calculation of the law. Before the final stampede toward the switch, a moment's hesitation is, comments the narrator, "long enough to reflect perhaps that it's too late, the Sabbath has already begun" (*PB*, 516). That is, it is too late to execute the sentence according to Jewish law. In this too-late time beyond the countdown, beyond calculable time, whatever happens cannot have been expected.

In the final lines of this final chapter (before the epilogue), the unexpected event is the public burning of Ethel Rosenberg who, as we already read, "unlike Saint Joan, will not be burned offstage—indeed, even had this been the plan, she would not have allowed it."

> Ethel Rosenberg's body, held only at head, groin, and one leg [because the assistants had started to unbuckle the restraints, believing she was dead—PK], is whipped like a sail in a high wind, flapping out at people like one of those trick images in a 3-D movie, making them scream and duck and pray for deliverance. Her body, sizzling and popping like firecrackers, lights up with the force of the current, casting a flickering radiance on all those around her, and so she burns—and burns—and burns—as though held aloft by her own incandescent will and haloed about by all the gleaming great of the nation— (*PB*, 517)

There would seem to be no less desecration ("her body, sizzling and popping like firecrackers") than consecration or sanctification (the body is "haloed") in this imagined end.[46] Yet one may read there a tribute to the "incandescent will" even in death, a will to live even in death, a will to survive not her death, which no mortal can, but to survive *in* death. Indeed, these lines are attesting to that unexpected survival by consecrating it in fiction. The light they cast is also cast back over the entirety of the novel as an act of historical

---

46. Of course, in the Epilogue that follows these last words of the penultimate chapter, consecration simply is desecration and vice versa because Nixon is invested, incarnated when Uncle Sam buggers him.

retrieval despite the enormity of its fictional inventions, of which these final lines give another example.

This chapter began with a pair of related questions: on the one hand, about the survival of the death penalty in the United States and, on the other, about the secrecy that this survival of the last of its kind increasingly relies on. The wager has been that the extravagant fiction of *The Public Burning*, by reversing the becoming-nonpublic of these two executions famous in U.S. history, may engage both of these questions. The Rosenberg affair was, of course, all about secrets, secrets stolen and passed to the enemy, secret proofs of treason held in FBI files, secret testimonies and conspiracies. The biggest secret of all, however, may have been that there was no secret.[47] That the secret is a nonsecret or that the true secret is a false secret. The secret that there is nothing to expose cannot itself be exposed because there is nothing to expose. And that is because it is not hidden but public, already public, in public. *The Public Burning*'s radical gesture, which transfers the stage of the executions, does not move from the hidden toward the public so much as it makes spectacularly public the already public. Its essential fiction, the transfer to Times Square, is the vehicle for thus *re-marking* the already public of the public. And what this fiction remarks is a public determined by "the real phenomena of the death penalty" (*DP I*, 258), these phenomena that are also psychic projections in a theater of cruelty. As such, this public also determines and demands the nonsecrecy of the death penalty wherever that practice persists by law.

But, finally, what is this "public," what is "the public," an entity

47. "Many of America's own atomic scientists . . . seem to be siding openly with the spies, claiming that there *is* no secret to the atom bomb in the first place . . ." (*PB*, 42); "And what is this that Dr. Urey and others are saying about there being no secret to the A-bomb in the first place?" (*PB*, 68); "True," reflects Nixon, "some of our own eggheads were contending . . . that there was no secret to the A-bomb, and that the Russians could have got more out of a Flash Gordon comic strip than out of Greenglass's famous diagrams" (*PB*, 302).

that is one, this one, e.g., the American public? Is the public in *The Public Burning* (noun plus adjective) one, all one, and just one? No, of course not, not really or only as a figure of speech or, better, as the very figure of and for public discourse—political, juridical, journalistic, popular. The "public" is a figure that exists only in and through speech or discourse. In this sense and for this reason, it is a fiction. For we know or want to believe we know that there are many "publics" who may be said (with another figure of speech) to burn: Some are burning with lust and desire, some are burning with shame, and some there are who burn—and burn—and burn for justice.

Plots carry their own logic. There is a tendency of plots to move toward death. He believed that the idea of death is woven into the nature of every plot. A narrative plot no less than a conspiracy of armed men. The tighter the plot of a story, the more likely it will come to death. A plot in fiction, he believed, is the way we localize the force of the death outside the book, play it off, contain it.

—Don DeLillo, *Libra*

THE SENTENCE IS THE STORY

Between 1968 and 1977, there were no executions in the United States. It is surprising to remember this fact today given that, since 1982, not a year has gone by without multiple executions in this country. During most of that earlier decade of *de facto* moratorium, there was considerable sentiment that the U.S. death penalty was finished.[1] To be sure, it was still on the books in many states, but as a law that was perhaps becoming the relic of a former age. However, at the beginning of the decade, in 1972, the U.S. Supreme Court chose not to rule the death penalty outright unconstitutional,[2] which would have converted *de facto* moratorium into *de jure* abolition. Instead, the court decided that, as currently applied, the death

1. See David Garland, *Peculiar Institution: America's Death Penalty in an Age of Abolition* (Cambridge, Mass.: The Belknap Press of Harvard University Press, 2010), chap. 8; David Oshinsky, *Capital Punishment on Trial: "Furman v. Georgia" and the Death Penalty in Modern America* (Lawrence: University of Kansas Press, 2010), chap. 2; Stuart Banner, *The Death Penalty: An American History* (Cambridge, Mass.: Harvard University Press, 2002), chap. 9.

2. In *Furman v. Georgia*, Justices William Brennan and Thurgood Marshall wrote separate, concurring opinions that also argued the unconstitutionality of the death penalty in general.

penalty contravened the Eighth and Fourteenth amendments.[3] This was the signal to all thirty-seven retentionist states to rewrite their penal codes, which they accordingly did, and by 1976, the Supreme Court was once again able to take up the question in order to approve the rewritten laws of several of them. *Gregg v. Georgia*, which bundled five such cases, all from Southern states (Georgia, Florida, Texas, North Carolina, Louisiana), provided the occasion for lifting the moratorium. It announced in effect that executions could resume, which they very quickly did.

This history is well enough known. I minimally rehearse it because it will be pertinent as context for reading the text that preoccupies this chapter, Norman Mailer's 1979 novel *The Executioner's Song*. When originally published, it was subtitled a "true life novel," but that odd designation has tended to disappear from subsequent editions and reissues. The novel was published just two years after the "true life" it chronicled, Gary Gilmore's, had been extinguished by firing squad in the Utah State Prison on January 17, 1977. The execution of Gilmore, a confessed and convicted murderer, was the first in the United States after *Gregg*, a dubious distinction achieved largely because Gilmore refused to appeal the death sentence handed down in October 1976, mere months after the enabling Supreme Court decision in *Gregg*.[4] Had he exercised his right to appeal, as he was urged to do by a succession of legal advisors, his case might well have challenged Utah's death penalty statute and

3. Garland writes of *Furman*: "It focused on procedure not substance, and on individual cases not general policies. . . . Far from a decisive abolition imposed by a self-confident elite, it was more like a tentative test balloon, floated by the Court to see how the political winds were blowing" (*Peculiar Institution*, 230); see also James Liebman, "Slow Dancing with Death: The Supreme Court and Capital Punishment, 1963–2006," *Columbia Law Review* 107 (2007): 1–130.

4. Gilmore was certainly not the first so-called volunteer for execution. Indeed, the last man executed pre-*Furman* also refused appeals (Luis Monge, Colorado, asphyxiation by gas, June 2, 1967). On some of the issues raised by this "volunteer syndrome," see Susan R. Schmeiser, "Waiving from Death Row," in *Who Deserves to Die?: Constructing the Executable Subject*, ed. Austin Sarat and Karl Shoemaker (Amherst: University of Massachusetts Press, 2011).

at least deferred, if not prevented, the resumption of capital punishment in the United States post-1976. As it happened, however, Gilmore challenged the people of Utah to have, as he cleverly put it, "the courage of their convictions" and put him to death: "Don't the people of Utah have the courage of their convictions?" wrote Gilmore to the Utah Supreme Court after it granted a stay of his execution against his own express wishes. "You sentence a man to die—me—and when I accept this most extreme punishment with grace and dignity, you, the people of Utah want to back down and argue with me. You're silly."[5]

The event that was Gary Gilmore's death as capital punishment resumes is recorded by *The Executioner's Song,* in which transcriptions of thousands of hours of interviews have been transformed with fictional license. The interviews were conducted with over a hundred persons, all of whom interacted with Gilmore in some way during the last nine months of his life. Seeming to adhere almost without a gap to the thoughts and feelings of its subjects, who are left largely to speak for themselves, the novel nevertheless transforms everything with its own work. This work is sometimes signaled by an "as if," for example: "It was as if somebody had hidden sparklers inside her heart in that place where she had expected to find nothing" (*ES,* 172). Or again: "She could feel the shock come over Pete as if he was bleeding inside over every part of him, past and present" (*ES,* 136). But more often the sounds and rhythms of speech simply carry over into this other medium, where they are repeated according to the fiction: "'Every day,' she said, 'is the same. It's all one day,' and nodded her head. 'You have to get them used up'" (*ES,* 227). My point is that this work of transformation—of writing—marks *The Executioner's Song* as fiction just as unmistakably as *The Public Burning,* which in a certain sense also adheres closely to "true life" inasmuch as it draws all of its characters from history.

5. Norman Mailer, *The Executioner's Song* (New York: Little, Brown, 1979), 542; hereafter *ES.*

Suspended as it is in the literary medium, the meaning of the event that was Gilmore's execution has been turned over by the novel to a future of reading that includes whatever we might discern from our own distance of forty years. Of course, in literary time forty years is not very significant, yet it gauges some dimension of the event that continues to happen here, now. It is the dimension, for example, in which punishment and ultimately the ultimate, capital punishment, work to displace whatever collective social drive there might have previously been to ameliorate social ills. *The Executioner's Song* records this displacement, as the logic of the "prison-industrial complex"[6] came to override belief in ideas such as rehabilitation, reeducation, resocialization, and racial integration. Mass incarceration (at the rate of 731 for every 100,000 inhabitants; "no other country even approaches that"),[7] especially of men of color; creation of a prison underclass; supermaxes; life without parole; mandatory sentencing; private prison management; massive use of solitary confinement; not to mention the numbers of men and women on death row—all of these indicators began to rise precipitously around 1976–1977.[8] Gilmore's despair at the prospect of life in prison, which is what he repeatedly claimed led him to elect execution, is something like a bellwether of this social catastrophe that was then in the making. When read from our dis-

6. This term was launched by Angela Davis in 1997. It was widely taken up and defined as "a set of bureaucratic, political, and economic interests that encourage increased spending on imprisonment, regardless of the actual need." Eric Schlosser, "The Prison-Industrial Complex," *Atlantic Monthly* (December 1998); http://www.theatlantic.com/magazine/archive/1998/12/the-prison-industrial-complex/304669/.

7. Adam Gopnik, "The Caging of America," *New Yorker*, January 30, 2012, http://www.newyorker.com/magazine/2012/01/30/the-caging-of-america.

8. According to the Justice Policy Institute's timeline, in 1976 there were 263,800 persons incarcerated in U.S. state and federal prisons; by 1986, the total had more than doubled (544,972). http://www.justicepolicy.org/uploads/justicepolicy/documents/jpi_poster. The U.S. Bureau of Justice Statistics counts 8,466 death sentences handed down between 1973 and 2013, of which 1,359 were carried out. U.S. Department of Justice, Tracy L. Snell, "Capital Punishment, 2013–Statistical Tables," December 2014; see also Michelle Alexander, *The New Jim Crow: Mass Incarceration in the Age of Colorblindness*, rev. ed. (New York: New Press, 2012).

tance, Mailer's novel can be seen to record this moment in U.S. penal history almost passively as it goes about its main task of telling the story of Gary Gilmore.

This story is also the story of its own becoming and proliferation as story (and finally as novel). The story of Gilmore's crimes and sentencing, as recounted in Book 1, "Western Voices," has a force of propagation that is chronicled in Book 2, "Eastern Voices." It is compelling in itself *as story*, as what is driven by narrative toward ending, the ending of a life as the end of story. Mailer has remarked that the recordings from which he worked had already the structure of a novel when they came into his hands:

> I was convinced from the start that the materials were exceptional; it had the structure of a novel. Whenever I needed a character for esthetic balance—a new character of imposing dimensions—one just appeared out of nowhere. If I had conceived *The Executioner's Song* as a novel entirely drawn from my own imagination, I doubt I could have improved on those characters.[9]

It is Gilmore's death by execution that confers this quality of finished narrative on his life. The Gary Gilmore story only begins when he is condemned to death; its value as story rises quickly after he refuses to appeal and keeps rising until he is executed. Long sections of "Eastern Voices" track this value on the media markets, the markets of Hollywood, broadcast TV (it is still the age of the networks), book publishing, magazines, and of course newspapers, from the local *Deseret News* in Salt Lake City to the largest papers in New York and Europe. These are the purveyors of narrative to the mainstream reading, watching, and paying public. All of this buying and selling of the story is part of the story as told in *The Executioner's Song*. It is told especially by Larry Schiller, the documentarian who not long after Gilmore's sentencing began taping interviews with witnesses. Interviews with Schiller himself about his different

---

9. Quoted in Carl E. Rollyson Jr., "Biography in a New Key," *Chicago Review* 31, no. 4 (Spring 1980): 34.

dealings with the various principals supply this material and reveal someone who is very canny about obtaining the rights to others' lives, that is, to their stories. Schiller, who shares the copyright of the novel, recruited Mailer to write it, which was yet another transaction in this story market.

That Gilmore's becomes a story only because he dies executed hardly needs to be pointed out. It seems self-evident enough to go without saying. This self-evidence points, I believe, to our fundamental relation to narrative or storytelling as relation to the end, to death.[10] That is, it is a relation also in the sense of telling, narrating, or relating stories. As Walter Benjamin explains in "The Storyteller," the authority of the story is located in the death from which a man's life "assumes transmissible form," the story to be repeated. Story is repetition of an unforgettable life that emerges from someone's death and "imparts to everything that concerned him that authority which even the poorest wretch in dying possesses for the living around him. This authority is at the very source of story."[11] Benjamin is here talking about the oral storytelling tradition, now largely disappeared in the industrialized West, where it has been displaced by written narratives, above all, the novel. Whereas storytelling happens in company with another, the novel reader, writes Benjamin, "is isolated, more so than any other reader." He does not explain right away why that should be so, but the rest of the passage gives some hints. I excerpt it at some length:

> It is dry material on which the burning of the reader feeds. "A man who dies at the age of thirty-five," said Moritz Heimann once, "is at every point of his life a man who dies at the age of thirty-five."

---

10. On narrative as end-oriented, see Frank Kermode, *The Sense of an Ending: Studies in the Theory of Fiction* (Oxford: Oxford University Press, 1966), esp. chap. 1, "The End"; and Peter Brooks, *Reading for the Plot: Design and Intention in Narrative* (New York: Knopf, 1984), chap. 1.

11. Walter Benjamin, "The Storyteller: Observations on the Work of Nikolai Leskov," trans. Harry Zohn, in *Selected Writings*, vol. 3, ed. Michael W. Jennings (Cambridge, Mass.: The Belknap Press of Harvard University Press, 2002), 156.

Nothing is more dubious than this sentence—but for the sole reason that the tense is wrong. A man—so says the truth that was meant here—who died at thirty-five will appear to *remembrance* at every point in his life as a man who dies at the age of thirty-five. In other words, the statement that makes no sense for real life becomes indisputable for remembered life. The nature of the character in a novel cannot be presented any better than is done in this statement, which says that the "meaning" of his life is revealed only in his death. But the reader of a novel actually does look for human beings from whom he derives the "meaning of life." Therefore he must, no matter what, know in advance that he will share their experience of death: if need be their figurative death—the end of the novel—but preferably their actual one. How do the characters make him understand that death is already waiting for them—*a very definite death and at a very definite place*? That is the question which feeds the reader's consuming interest in the events of the novel. (156; emphases added)

It would seem that the reader of a novel is more alone than any other because the experience sets him before his death, the one that cannot be known in advance by him but only afterward by others and as remembrance. But the novel can appear to give him an experience of death and grant a "meaning of life" contained by its end. The novel's characters will all die a prescripted death, if only figuratively by expiring with the end of the novel, and it is with this certainty that the novel's reader advances, trying to grasp "the meaning of life" in advance of the death that alone can confer it. He reads, Benjamin remarks, "in the hope of warming his shivering life with a death he reads about" (101). Or as Don DeLillo puts it in our epigraph, "a plot in fiction . . . is the way we localize the force of the death outside the book, play it off, contain it."[12] We localize it, as Benjamin would have it, "at a very definite place."

---

12. Kermode acknowledges that today only the most trivial fiction follows this pattern of strict plotting from the end. Modernists broke with the pattern by multiplying peripætia and plotless succession (see Kermode, *The Sense of an Ending*, esp. chap. 4). And indeed,

If I am construing Benjamin plausibly, then there are some further implications specifically for a novel like *The Executioner's Song*, that is, one that has a death penalty plot. Indeed, Benjamin may almost be heard claiming that every novel's characters are subject to a death penalty insofar as they make readers understand "that death is already waiting for them—a very definite death and at a very definite place." This definiteness arises from the definition of the end—its finition, if you will, the limit that, according to Benjamin, defines the novel. After quoting the last lines of Flaubert's *Sentimental Education*, he comments:

> With such an insight the novel reaches an end which is more proper to it, in a stricter sense, than to any story. Actually there is no story for which the question "How did it continue?" would not be legitimate. The novelist, on the other hand, cannot hope to take the smallest step beyond that limit at which he invites the reader to a divinatory realization of the meaning of life by writing "Finis." (155)[13]

This, then, is the de-finition that confers "a very definite death and at a very definite place" on the novel's characters, as vicariously experienced by a reader looking for the meaning of life that is revealed only in death. Plotted narrative thus has essentially a death penalty plot, in which knowledge of a defined end precedes this end and determines a story that only seems to lead to it but will in fact have been plotted from and by the end. If Gilmore's death by execution can confer the quality of story on the more or less random events and incidents retold in "Western Voices," that is because it decides the story's beginning and middle in function of its end

---

Benjamin seems to be talking above all about dime-store novels. Brooks, likewise, concludes his study of principally nineteenth-century novels with an epilogue that observes of modernist and postmodernist fiction: "Our most sophisticated literature understands endings to be artificial, arbitrary, minor rather than major chords, casual and textual rather than cosmic and definitive" (314).

13. Curiously, Mailer observes this now more or less obsolete practice at the end of his novel.

and the execution of the sentence. It confers narrative structure, or what Mailer recognizes as the structure of a novel. And that structure is essentially teleological, plotted from an end.

In her very admiring and astute review of *The Executioner's Song*, Joan Didion calls Mailer "a writer to whom the shape of the sentence is the story."[14] Paying attention to this shape, she isolates a long sentence that stands out against the simple, featureless sentences that make up so much of the novel. This sentence comes at the end of the first chapter, and it registers the moment when Brenda, Gary's cousin, learns that he is getting out of prison and would soon be arriving in Salt Lake from Marion, Illinois, traveling through St. Louis and then Denver:

> With all the excitement Brenda was hardly taking into account that
> it was practically the same route their Mormon great-grandfather
> took when he jumped off from Missouri with a handcart near to a
> hundred years ago, and pushed west with all he owned over the
> prairies, and the passes of the Rockies, to come to rest at Provo in the
> Mormon Kingdom of Deseret just fifty miles below Salt Lake. (*ES* 10)

Didion comments that "the relative complexity and length of this sentence . . . is a chill, a signal that the author is telling us a story of some historical dimension." And indeed, Gary's story begins to unfold as such when it starts to repeat the ancestral journey, which like any journey that reaches a destination will have had a beginning, middle, and an end. Gary's story begins by repeating the history of Mormon migration. The "historical dimension" that Didion remarks inscribes this repetition in the general structure of narrative, which, as I have been suggesting, shares the structure of a death sentence. *The Executioner's Song* is the story of stories because it is propelled by the essence of narrative, which is the execu-

14. Joan Didion, "'I Want to Go Ahead and Do It,'" *New York Times Book Review*, October 7, 1979, http://www.nytimes.com/books/97/05/04/reviews/mailer-song.html.

tion of a death sentence. In this sense as well, then, for Mailer "the sentence is the story," to recall Didion's phrase.

Mailer's novel thus bids one to consider general questions about narrative, story, and death penalty. Yet it is anything but a generic death penalty novel, supposing there could be such a thing.[15] Gilmore is particularized, specified, made excruciatingly singular by the time he faces his executioners at the end. Which does not prevent (on the contrary) that he comes to occupy a universal position before the law that has condemned him. Like Kafka's man from the country, who thinks "the Law should be accessible at all times and to everyone" but who has to stand before the Law's gate that "was made only for [him],"[16] Gilmore is put to death by the law meant for everyone yet gated by the singular limit of his own finitude. Or as Jacques Derrida has put it in his remarkable essay on Kafka's parable, "There is a singularity about relationship to the law, a law of singularity, which must come into contact with the general or universal essence of the law without ever being able to do so."[17]

But the novel has more than this general claim on our interest. It also captures and displays a kind of knot or loophole in the logic of the death penalty or even of punishment in general. To put it in simple terms, which we will have to refine, Gilmore's taunting the law to have the courage of its convictions and calling it "silly" signal toward the way the law of punishment can fail to punish, even or especially when it decides to impose the maximum punishment. And

---

15. Victor Hugo did attempt to do just that in his *Last Day of a Condemned Man*. In the 1832 Preface to his novel, he explains that the condemned man is unnamed because the author wished "to plead the case of any condemned man whatsoever, executed on any day whatsoever, for any crime whatsoever. Victor Hugo, *Écrits sur la peine de mort* (Arles: Actes Sud, 1979), 10.

16. Franz Kafka, "Before the Law," in *The Penal Colony: Stories and Short Pieces*, trans. Willa and Edwin Muir (New York: Schocken, 1948), 148, 150.

17. Jacques Derrida, "Before the Law," trans. Avital Ronell, in *Acts of Literature*, ed. Derek Attridge (New York: Routledge, 1992), 187.

this possibility prompts one to ask the apparently absurd but none-theless serious question: Did Gary Gilmore indeed die executed by capital punishment, or did his death deprive the sovereign law of certainty as to its ultimate power over life and death?

As caught in the fixative of the novel, Gilmore's story raises or poses this question, and first of all to the law itself, that is, to its rep-resentatives. Consider in this regard Gilmore's hearing before the Utah Board of Pardons a month after his sentencing. The hearing took place because the governor of the state, Calvin Rampton, had issued a stay of execution and instructed the Board of Pardons to rule on whether the death sentence was justified. Cutting between excerpts from the hearing transcript and the recorded accounts of several witnesses who had been present, the novel frames the event of the hearing as a verbal wrestling match between Gilmore (whom one of the witnesses reflects "could have been a graduate student going for his orals before a faculty of whom he was slightly con-temptuous" [*ES*, 698]) and the several representatives of the law or the state there to argue and to hear the case. Gilmore is given the floor first:

> "I am wondering," he began by saying. "Your Board dispenses
> privilege, and I have always thought that privileges were sought,
> desired, earned and deserved, and I seek nothing from you, don't
> desire anything from you, haven't earned anything and I don't
> deserve anything either." (*ES* 699)

At the outset, then, the proceeding is confronted with Gilmore's desire, albeit expressed as a lack of desire—"I seek nothing from you, don't desire anything from you"—for the privilege the Board of Pardons alone can decide to dispense or withhold. As a conse-quence, this power to decide, which is also the power to punish, becomes unsettled, gets thrown off balance by the one brought before it whose will is nevertheless to submit to the law. It is as if this submission to the law had somehow managed to step outside its purview. This becomes clear as the exchange between Gilmore and the chairman of the Board of Pardons continues. First Gilmore:

> I had come to the conclusion that because of Utah's Governor Rampton, I was here, because he bowed to whatever pressures were on him.
>
> I had personally decided he was a moral coward for doing it. *I simply accepted the sentence that was given to me.* I have accepted sentences all my life. I didn't know I had a choice in the matter.
>
> When I did accept it, everybody jumped up and wanted to argue with me. It seems that the people, especially the people of Utah, want the death penalty but they don't want executions and when it became a reality they might have to carry one out, well, they started backing off on it.
>
> Well I took them literal and serious when they sentenced me to death just as if they had sentenced me to ten years or thirty days in the county jail or something. I thought you were supposed to take them serious. I didn't know it was a joke. . . . *It's by courts that I die and I accept that.* . . . (*ES*, 699–700; emphases added)

The final ellipsis, which is in the text, indicates perhaps that the chairman interrupts Gilmore here and not without what sounds like some exasperation: "CHAIRMAN: Now, in spite of what you may think about us, you can rest assured that we are not cowards, and you can rest assured that we are going to decide this case on the statutes of the State of Utah and not your desires" (*ES,* 700). But such assurances notwithstanding, Gilmore's desires have already intruded themselves onto the grounds of decision, which start to slip out from under the feet of these brave officials. For the specter has been raised that the state is merely following the condemned man's desire rather than imposing its sentence on him.

This specter materializes in the remarks of the next to speak, Richard Giauque. Giauque is a lawyer who will later file a Next Friend petition in the U.S. Supreme Court, which will then, and once again over Gilmore's objections, issue another stay of execution. But meanwhile back in the Board of Pardons hearing, Giauque takes the floor and has to point out several times that Gilmore's desire is not relevant or "paramount" to the question at issue:

> Society has an interest in this wholly apart from Mr. Gilmore's wishes. I do think that there are some facts here that ought to be looked into. One of them is whether or not he has voluntarily waived his legal rights, or whether or not he is asking the State merely to become an accomplice. . . . It is not Mr. Gilmore's desire that is paramount here and I would merely ask, Mr. Chairman, . . . that the decision to utilize the death sentence not be made by Mr. Gilmore and not be made by this Board, but . . . be resolved by the Courts.
> (*ES*, 701; ellipses in the text)

Giauque formulates the question quite pointedly: In asking "whether or not [Gilmore] is asking the State merely to become an accomplice," the lawyer is warning that the condemned may be using the state to end his life, to commit, as it were, suicide by court. On this hypothesis, his apparent submission ("I simply accepted the sentence that was given to me," "It's by the courts I die and I accept that") would be but a ruse to hijack the execution to his own end, in both the teleological and eschatological senses. In his brief to the Board of Pardons, a short portion of which is quoted two chapters later, Giauque is more direct: Gilmore, he affirms, "is, in fact, choosing to commit suicide":

> Allowing a defendant to waive judicial review of a death sentence . . . is tantamount to committing suicide.[18] The Talmud, Aristotle, Augustine, and Aquinas all characterize suicide as a grievous private and public wrong. At common law, suicide was held as a felony, and was attended by forfeiture of property and burial on the highway. . . . A criminal defendant such as Gilmore, who declines to pursue legal

---

18. Because the ellipsis in this sentence is in the text, there is no way to tell if the full sentence managed to avoid the syntactic implication that it is the state or the law that commits suicide.

proceedings which could save his life is, in fact, choosing to commit suicide, and the overwhelming majority of psychiatric opinion regards the impulse to suicide as a form of mental illness. (*ES*, 730; ellipses in the text)

Giauque is mobilizing all of these authorities—the Talmud, Aristotle, church fathers, common law, and finally modern psychiatry—in the interest, first of all, of overturning Gilmore's sentence but also and beyond that of slowing the return of the death penalty regime post-*Gregg* and, in the longer run, of building toward abolition. As a lawyer associated with the ACLU, Richard Giauque had these objectives in mind no doubt when he urged that "society has an interest in this wholly apart from Mr. Gilmore's wishes." Likewise, Anthony Amsterdam, the noted abolition activist law professor working with the NAACP Legal Defense Fund who argued *Furman v. Georgia*, was agitating in the wings to help overturn Gilmore's sentence.

To no avail, of course. And given that Gary Gilmore did indeed die by firing squad as ordered by the state of Utah, one might well say it little matters whether that death is called an execution or a suicide. Yet the issue was important enough to draw the attention and vigorous argument of no less than Immanuel Kant, whom Derrida in his *Death Penalty* seminar repeatedly characterizes as fielding the most rigorous philosophical argument in support of capital punishment, which Kant referred to as "the categorical imperative of penal law."[19] In the several pages of *The Metaphysics of Morals* devoted to "The Right to Punish and to Grant Clemency" (in *The Doctrine of Right*, II, Remark E), Kant confronts exactly this issue of state-imposed capital punishment versus the will to die of the one punished. Reviewing that argument now should help us gauge better the implications of Gilmore's challenge to his judges.

---

19. See Jacques Derrida, *The Death Penalty, Volume I*, ed. Geoffrey Bennington and Thomas Dutoit, trans. Peggy Kamuf (Chicago: University of Chicago Press, 2013), 124–127, 271–273; hereafter *DP I*. See also Geoffrey Bennington, "Rigor: Or Stupid Uselessness," *Southern Journal of Philosophy* 50, Spindel Supplement (2012).

Having first deduced the principle of the *lex talionis* and the "fitting of punishment to the crime" that dictates the requirement of the death penalty in the penal code, and then having pronounced, categorically and imperatively, "If, however, he [the wrongdoer] has committed murder he must *die*,"[20] Kant takes up the counterargument of Cesare Beccaria, whose *Dei delitti e della pene* (*Of Crimes and Punishments*) had been published a little more than twenty years earlier in 1764 and quickly translated and circulated throughout Europe. Kant has no patience at all with Beccaria's "overly compassionate" plea to end the practice of capital punishment:

> In opposition to this the Marchese Beccaria, moved by overly compassionate feelings of an affected humanity (*compassibilitas*), has put forward his assertion that any capital punishment is wrongful because it could not be contained in the original civil contract; for if it were, everyone in a people would have to have consented to lose his life in case he murdered someone else (in the people), whereas it is impossible for anyone to consent to this because no one can dispose of his own life. (*MM*, 108)

"This is all sophistry and juristic trickery," fulminates Kant. He then proceeds to show how Beccaria has gone astray (above all, perhaps, as a reader of Rousseau's *Social Contract*, although Kant leaves that aside). To set things right, the philosopher needs just one medium-length paragraph, which begins: "No one suffers punishment because he has willed *it* but because he has willed a *punishable action*; for it is no punishment if what is done to someone is what he wills, and it is impossible *to will* to be punished." Kant thus goes straight to the dilemma that Gilmore's judges and legal opponents were struggling to resolve: If what is done to someone is what he or she wills, then it is not punishment.

If "it is impossible *to will* to be punished," that is because, Kant

---

20. Immanuel Kant, *The Metaphysics of Morals*, ed. and trans. Mary Gregor (Cambridge: Cambridge University Press, 1996), 106; hereafter *MM*.

explains, the one who makes the law and the one who breaks it cannot be the same person, even if he is the same person. Here is how he explains this apparent riddle:

> Saying that I will to be punished if I murder someone is saying nothing more than that I subject myself together with everyone else to the laws, which will naturally also be penal laws if there are any criminals among the people.[21] As a co-legislator in dictating the penal law, I *cannot possibly be the same person* who, as a subject, is punished in accordance with the law; for as one who is punished, namely as a criminal, I cannot possibly have a voice in legislation (the legislator is holy). Consequently, when I draw up a penal law against myself as a criminal, it is pure reason in me (*homo noumenon*), legislating with regard to rights, which subjects me, as someone capable of crime and *so as another person* (*homo phænomenon*), to the penal law, together with all others in a civil union. (MM, 108; emphases added)

Kant could thus reassure Gilmore's judges that the one they punish is the *homo phænomenon*, not to be confused with the *homo noumenon* in the same individual who can will punishment and therefore can in effect will his own death, or rather the death of the *homo phænomenon* he harbors (or who harbors him if the latter is guilty of murder). Another way to state this is that *homo noumenon* cannot be punished, but it can will punishment—of the other, phenomenal man. Or yet again, that there is a will to punish, but "it is impossible to *will* to be punished." The paragraph concludes by pointing out that the "chief point of error" of Beccaria's sophistry

> consists in its confusing the criminal's own judgment (which must necessarily be ascribed to his *reason*) that he has to forfeit his life

---

21. This conditional clause rather touchingly suggests that Kant supposes the possibility of a people without any criminals, even potential ones. On this Kantian supposition of a fully rational polity that would not even need a criminal code, see *DP*, 271–273; and Bennington, "Rigor," 35.

> with a resolve on the part of his *will* to take his own life, and so in
> representing as united in one and the same person the judgment
> upon a right and the realization of that right. (MM, 108)

In sum, then, Kant simply rules out of court the dilemma that
ensnared Gilmore's judges and advocates like Giauque. They, like
Beccaria, confused the condemned man's judgment, which had accepted the sentence, with the will to take his own life. They confused, in other words, *homo noumenon* with *homo phænomenon*.
What they did not realize is that the slightly contemptuous Gilmore
was, however unknowingly, a student of Kant. Channeling his inner
homo noumenon, he could thus affirm before the Utah Supreme
Court: "I desire to be executed on schedule and I just wish to accept
that with the grace and dignity of a man" (*ES*, 556). That dignity is
what Kant would have called *Würde*, the worth or worthiness that
is not just above price and market but above even the value of life.
For, as Derrida writes, channeling his inner Kant, "no law will ever
be founded on an unconditional love of life for its own sake, on the
absolute refusal of any sacrifice of life" (*DP I*, 128).

What Kant seems most intent to dispute and dispel in his tiff with
Beccaria, then, is the latter's implied conflation of the death penalty
with suicide. This is likewise the point that rubs on the judges and
advocates in the Gilmore case. So when is a legal execution a suicide? Is it even possible to determine this? Whereas Kant would denounce that question as supposing an error—which "consists in . . .
confusing the criminal's own judgment . . . with a resolve on the
part of his will to take his own life"—Derrida locates just this distinction between suicide and execution as one place where Kant's logic
of the death penalty (whose possibility "belongs to the structure
of the law")[22] is untenable in all rigor. As he relates in an interview
published in 2001:

---

22. "In any case, the possibility of the death penalty, that is, of the law as what raises *homo
noumenon* above *homo phaenomenon* (above its empirical life), belongs to the structure of
the law." *DP I*, 127.

The "deconstruction" I am trying to carry out in my seminar [on the death penalty] would make . . . appear untenable, from within . . . the distinction between self-punishment and hetero-punishment: the guilty party, as a person and a rational subject, should, according to Kant, understand, approve, even call for the punishment—including the supreme penalty. . . . To follow this consequence to the end, the guilty party would symbolically execute the verdict himself. The execution would be like a *sui-cide*. There would be, for the autonomy of juridical reason, nothing but self-execution. It is "as if the guilty party committed suicide."[23]

Gilmore resembles to a T the rational subject who "should, according to Kant, understand, approve, even call for the punishment." For example, right after his arrest, when Gary has confessed his murder to a police lieutenant, he calls for his own execution:

"I hope they execute me for what I did."
  "Gary, are you ready to?" Nielsen asked. "It doesn't scare you?"
  "Would you like to die?"
  "Criminy," said Nielsen, "no."
  "Me neither," said Gilmore, "but I ought to be executed for it."
(*ES,* 309)

According to Kant in his response to Beccaria, "saying that I will to be punished if I murder someone is saying nothing more than that I subject myself together with everyone else to the laws": Notice how the phrase "nothing more," "nichts mehr," holds at bay the specter of execution-as-suicide and what Derrida calls "self-execution." Yet, as fashioned by Kant the rational subject accepts the principle whereby "whatever undeserved evil you inflict upon another within the people, that you inflict upon yourself" and specifies that "if you kill him, you kill yourself" (*MM,* 105). In other words, your crime is equal to your punishment. This principle of equality is at the root of the *lex talionis* and thus of the death penalty, the only punish-

23. Jacques Derrida and Elisabeth Roudinesco, *For What Tomorrow . . . A Dialogue,* trans. Jeff Fort (Stanford, Calif.: Stanford University Press, 2004), 150.

THE SENTENCE IS THE STORY

ment fitting and equal to the crime of murder. Yet Kant's principle of equality, according to which murder = death penalty, cannot ultimately exorcise the other equation according to which death penalty = suicide. Murder, execution, suicide: These three deaths are necessarily suspended together within, as Derrida puts it, the "credit we grant to the word 'death'":

> The calculable credit we grant to the word "death" is indexed to a set of presuppositions, a network of presuppositions in which "capital punishment," the calculation of capital punishment, finds its place of inscription where it is indissociable from both murder and suicide.
> (*DP I*, 239)

I would like to return to my earlier suggestion that Mailer's novel gives us the gauge of an event that, in a sense, began to happen with Gilmore's execution in 1977 and is still defining our era as post-*Gregg*, that is, the era initiated by the resumption of capital punishment in the United States. Because it is still our era, we do not know how to measure it; we do not know if it is at an end or if its ending will go on ending, without end. Ours is the strange era of the end of the death penalty, which is the end of a certain way of life's ending. But it is also perhaps or even certainly the era of the survival of this mode of death, for example, in the penalty of life without the possibility of parole (LWPP), a life sentence that is a death sentence, the promise of death in prison, albeit no longer at a time determined by the state. The 2016 California Ballot Initiative sponsored under the name "Justice That Works" is just one example of proposed legislation against the death penalty that offered the alternative sentence of LWPP in its place. Therefore, to endorse this initiative to end the death penalty in California (which has the largest death row population in the country: 743)[24] was also to endorse its survival in a

---

24. According to the Death Penalty Information Center: http://www.deathpenaltyinfo.org/state_by_state.

post-post-*Gregg* era, the era of LWPP and mass incarceration.[25] As
Derrida might say, this is not a difference but a differance that also
defers, puts off, and suspends the difference between the sentence of life and the sentence of death. No less suspended is the
end or death of the death penalty. This suspended condition affects the whole post-*Gregg* era, beginning with the very execution,
Gilmore's, that signaled the revival, resurrection, or rebirth in the
United States of capital punishment. Yet since it marks a new beginning for ending (life) in this way—but actually in an entirely new
way, since *Gregg* also recognized the "humaneness" of lethal injection, which became the execution mode of choice throughout the
country—it also put this ending at the beginning.

I have used these terms to set up an echo with the narrative
structure that, as we have seen and as Benjamin, Kermode, Brooks,
and other narratologists assert, unfolds from the end at the beginning. This is the structure exhibited in and by *The Executioner's
Song*, but with that title Mailer is also conferring a poetic name on
what was just then starting to unfold as the post-*Gregg* era. That is,
it gives poetic measure of the event that was the revival of the U.S.
death penalty. In calling this name or this measure poetic, I do not
mean only that the novel's style or writing is poetic but also that
its title quotes the title of a poem, "The Executioner's Song," that
Mailer first published in 1964 and again in a collection in 1966.[26]
Like the "old prison rhyme" set in epigraph to the novel,[27] "the executioner's song" could very well be the name of a traditional prison
ballad. Nevertheless, it is a striking phrase, and it is striking as well

25. The ballot initiative failed in the November 2016 election.
26. The poem first appeared in the magazine *Fuck You* in September 1964. Its republication was in Norman Mailer, *Cannibals and Christians* (New York: Dial, 1966), 131–132. All references here are to the latter edition.
27. This eight-line epigraph (which is Mailer's invention) is reprised and extended by a second eight-line stanza as the final words of the text, just before "FINIS." According to David Guest, Mailer originally wrote the lines for his film *Maidstone* in the 1960s; see Guest, *Sentenced to Death*, 155.

that it never occurs in the novel itself.[28] Thus the title refers to the work as a whole rather than to any one of its parts. It is the novel as such that is or that sings the executioner's song. But the reprise of the title of the poem is intriguing. What did this poem say that Mailer wanted to repeat and reinscribe fifteen years later?

Here are the first of the poem's fifty-odd lines:

> I think if I had three good years to give
>   in study at some occupation
>   which was fierce and new
>   and full of stimulation
> I think I would become
>   an executioner
>   with time spent out in the field
>   digging graves for bodies I had made
>   the night before.

The next line moves to explain the wish to "become an executioner" but also a gravedigger, and this movement of explanation will carry the poem to its end. Indeed, the poem is all about the end, ends, and endings, as remarked in the next line: "You see: I am bad at endings." What does that mean, to be "bad at endings"? And how does it motivate the desire to become an executioner? By way of explanation, there tumble through the next few lines images of the speaker's bowels that "move without honor," of the affliction of flatulence, and of "much too much" preoccupation with sex. This sounds like adolescent, scatological humor, where "bad at endings" is associated right away with the rear end, the hind end, and the lower parts. But the stanza's last two lines elicit another way to hear all this embarrassed explanation:

> Those who end well do not spend their time
>   so badly on the throne

---

28. It does occur in the "Afterword," where Mailer describes how the novel came about.

Besides its scatological allusion, this aphorism might be a warning to sovereigns seated on some throne or other to spend their time well if they would end well. But, again, what does it mean "to end well"? Is it talking about an intransitive ending of life or a transitive one, a life that has been ended, and ended well, by the skillful executioner? Can they be separated out from each other, or are they somehow inextricable? This is, I believe, what the poem is asking itself or trying to learn. The question carries through to the poem's end in lines that echo the aphoristic quality of those I have just quoted. As we will hear, these final lines pronounce (and aphorisms always pronounce a truth) not just on ending well but on the best ending.

The poem, then, would arrive at this best of ends by learning, as it puts it, "to kill well and to bury well":

> I could execute neatly
>   (with respect for whatever romantic
>   imagination
> gave passion to my subject's crime)
> and if I buried well
> (with tenderness, dispatch, gravity
> and joy that the job was not jangled—
> giving a last just touch of the spade to the coffin
>   in order to leave it
> quivering
>   like a leaf—for forget not
> coffins quiver as the breath goes out
> and the earth comes down)

It is as if fifteen years later *The Executioner's Song* (the novel, soon to be a film)[29] had realized this wish: a neat execution that respects the subject's (Gilmore's) romantic imagination and, in its ultimate chapters, buries well, "with tenderness, dispatch, gravity," the spade

---

29. The 1982 made-for-TV film was directed by Lawrence Schiller with a screenplay by Mailer. Tommy Lee Jones plays Gary Gilmore.

now represented by the writer's tool that leaves Gilmore's remains "quivering like a leaf" as his ashes are dropped over Utah. Such a rapprochement of poem and novel makes apparent the writer's or the poet's role as executioner. The song is his, and the writer wants to execute, that is *end*, his or her characters well. By itself, then, this stanza could motivate the repetition of the title of the poem in the title of the novel. Which would motivate in turn our interpretive choice to read the poem through the wide lens of the novel but also the novel through the elliptical lens of the poem.

Meanwhile the poem itself is not about becoming a novel in fifteen years but an executioner in three ("if I had three good years to give/in study at some occupation"). What are the occupation-specific skills of an executioner? The poem gives us only two adverbs to go on: "neatly" in the line "I could execute neatly" and "cleanly" in the later line "Yes, if I could kill cleanly." They denote perhaps the prime skill of the executioner: delivering a swift, unequivocal end, a clean cut made between life and death, which should be drawn with the neatness of a straight one-dimensional line and without any grey area where life lingers in death and vice versa. Clearly, however, it is not or not just a technical skill that the poem attributes to the executioner: he must also and first of all see to the living and the dead with respect, compassion, tenderness, gravity, and then finally, in the end, he must see a living man die, or rather he must let a man about to die (by his hand) see him as "what is last to be seen/in his eye." Here are the lines of the last stanza that lead up to this image:

Yes, if I could kill cleanly
    and learn not to turn my back
    on the face of each victim
    as he chooses
        what is last to be seen
    in his eye, . . .

This last exchange of looks with the victim is positioned by the poem as the summit of the executioner's achievement, but also of poetic creation, which the ambition of becoming an executioner was always meant to serve, feed, and stimulate. For has not the poet all along been dreaming of becoming an executioner so that he might become a better poet? The summit where these ambitions meet, as on a mountain pass, is this passage of looks, when living and dying exchange glances.[30] That this is the height of poetic creation as well as of the executioner's craft is affirmed as the stanza continues from this hypothetical encounter with the face of death, which leads to the creation or procreation of poems:

> then might I rise so high upon occasion
> as to smite a fist of the Lord's creation
> into the womb of that muse
> which gives us poems
> Yes then I might

The rhyming couplet—"occasion/creation"—of those first two lines (the only one in the poem) signals the thought transfer from the executioner back to the poet whose wish or desire originally set everything in motion. Beside this end rhyme, "might" and "smite" form an internal rhyme that aligns them and reinforces the one with the other, might with smite, smite with might. And this mighty fist might smite a womb, for "then might I rise so high/. . . Yes then I might." Is the poem outlining a cure for erectile dysfunction? But no, it seems not, at least not according to some lines I omitted earlier where remedy is sought for a different malfunction:

> I would like to kill well and bury well
> Perhaps then my seed would not shoot
>   so frantic a flare

In addition to its sexual allusion, this frantic flare of shooting seed can always be a metaphor for the failed poetic act. That sense is re-

---

30. In fact, the lines speak only of a possible exchange of glances. What the executioner has to learn is to let his own face or eyes be *chosen* as "what is last to be seen/in his eye." The exchange of looks is only hypothetical but not for that any less difficult to master.

inforced when, in the poem's final stanza, we get the image of some
kind of triumph, at least a possible one, for "might" also speaks of
possibility rather than any certain realization. And this possible triumph is thrust like a fist into the womb of "that muse/who gives us
poems." Thus, what might come about is a poetico-sexual triumph
(and a brutal one, a rape even) over the muse of endings, who deliv-
ers the poem, gives it to the poet like his child.

I call her the muse of endings because the poet's quest to learn
to end well, that is, to execute neatly and cleanly, leads him to her,
as if she could deliver not just the good end but the best end. The
poem leaves this best end for last, in the final lines that echo the
earlier aphorism ("Those who end well do not spend their time/so
badly on the throne"):

> For one ends best when death is clean
>   to the mind
>   and calm in its proportions
> fire in the orchard and flames at the root

Like the previous aphorism, this one is suspended from the question of what "to end" means: the intransitive end that is one's own
mortal end? Or the transitive end that the executioner-poet "neatly"
and "cleanly" gives to the other's life by ending it in what is called
an execution? "For one ends best when death is clean/to the mind":
this end would be clean like a concept but also clean like an execution. Indeed, the concept should even be thought to presup-
pose the belief in the clean death that the figure of execution and
the executioner procures for it, in the mind if not always—or even
ever—in practice. In this way, the poem would indicate the place of
execution within what we mean by death, the end, ending well or
badly, and, if you can believe in such a thing, the best end.

I will offer just one last speculation about how the poem and
the novel are reading each other. The fifteen years that separated
them encompass the period of *de facto* moratorium from 1968 to
1977. In 1964, when the poem was first published, the number of
executions in the United States had begun to drop off sharply, and

during 1966, when the poem was collected by Mailer in *Canni-bals and Christians*, there was only one execution (James French, white male, for murder, by electrocution in Oklahoma).[31] Can the poem be seen to correlate in some way to this pre-*Furman* experi-ence in the era of a vanishing death penalty? I would say that yes, it does, and that this has to do with the paradox I pointed to above, whereby the end of the death penalty calls up the figure of its sur-vival in another form or guise, like LWPP. "The Executioner's Song" implicates death by execution in the very idea of end and in the con-cept of death "clean to the mind." It thus points to the repetition of some death penalty whenever death—of whatever sort, by whatever means—is invoked. If one has a concept of death, it is because the death penalty is inscribed within it. Thus, the poem invokes this repetition even as the death penalty was coming to an end, or so it seemed, in this country.

One last remark regarding the poem's pre-*Furman* perspective, as I just called it. This perspective is also necessarily pre-*Gregg*, and in that respect, the poem's aphoristic bent might even be heard an-ticipating our era's compulsive search for how best to end the lives of those condemned to death. The search certainly did not begin with *Furman v. Georgia*, but this decision gave it a particular impe-tus and direction that was going to lead to lethal injection and to the post-*Gregg* era, the "modern era," as many call it, of the American death penalty. I would even go so far out on this limb as to say that Mailer's poem anticipates lethal injection or at least the necessity that it be invented. It does so above all in those penultimate lines: "For one ends best when death is clean/to the mind/and calm in its proportions." A clean and calm death, is that not the dream of the post-*Gregg* death penalty, which is "humane" and neither cruel nor unusual? It would be clean, even antiseptic in the simulated surgical theater of the death chamber, and calm because the lethal

---

31. From DeathPenaltyUsa, http://deathpenaltyusa.org/usa1/date/1966.htm.

drug cocktail will be based on an anesthetic, such that when forced to reformulate their protocols, the various state departments of corrections will always look first for a substitute anesthetic.

"For one ends best . . ." says the aphorism. Gary Gilmore chose death by firing squad. Before a hood covered his head, he is described in *The Executioner's Song* looking and speaking for one of the very last times:

> Then the Warden said, "Do you have anything you'd like to say?" and Gary looked up at the ceiling and hesitated, then said, "Let's do it." That was it. The most pronounced amount of courage, Vern decided, he'd ever seen, no quaver, no throatiness, right down the line. *Gary had looked at Vern as he spoke.* (*ES*, 1016; emphasis added)

A few paragraphs later Gilmore's life ends or is ended, suicide or execution, put to death, as we say, by the squad of men whose screened eyes and faces he will never have seen. And in this end we hear the executioner's song start up again.

The poem, however, bids to have the last word. For its pronouncement on the best end (such as, in his uncle Vern's words, "The most pronounced amount of courage . . . he'd ever seen") is succeeded or supplemented by a final line: "fire in the orchard and flames at the root." It is a regular and symmetrical decasyllable that, at the very end of the poem, seems to assert nothing more (and nothing less) than elliptical, allusive poetic diction in the face of death delivered cleanly and calmly, by firing squad if you will, like a truth pronounced aphoristically, apodictically. But as nothing in the poem seems to connect to this fire and these flames,[32] the line is left dangling at the end, before the end, or perhaps already beyond the end.

---

32. Except via this alliteration that recalls both "so frantic a flare" in line 23 and, in line 3, "fierce." Or even the poem's first place of publication, *Fuck You: A Magazine of the Arts*.

5

PLAYING THE LAW

Throughout its chapters this book has been trying to configure various relations between literature—or some literary works—and the death penalty. These have included the relation that the witness bears to the act insofar as s/he must give the testimony that the sentence requires in order to be executed *as* death penalty. Orwell's brief story of a witnessed hanging was accordingly read as evidence of the poetic invention of testimony that, ambiguously and at once, both disturbs all conviction in the justice of the sentence and enables it to be carried out as a death sentence. Yet, *as* literature, that is, as a published, reprinted, and reread text, Orwell's story ends up weighting this ambiguity largely toward its own suspended conviction, one that hangs on the condemned man's sidestep to avoid a puddle in the road. The next configuration, drawn from *The Public Burning*, enlarges upon the irreducible role of the witness in the age of secrecy surrounding executions, which arguably began in Europe around the time, in the mid–nineteenth century, that John Stuart Mill reflected on the advisedness of moving capital

executions in Britain out of public view.[1] Coover's novel entails, as
its central fiction, a reversal of this becoming-secret or becoming-
hidden of the death penalty in the West. This fictional publicness
or publicity is thus the *doing* of the novel and of the claim of the
literary to uncensored and unfettered publication. That the brief
history of publication of *The Public Burning* has been anything but
unfettered, including a period when it was out of print, points one
perhaps to the limit at which a literary text can provoke the law,
bring out the suppositions of its legitimacy, and mark out a space
of fundamental contestation. In contrast, the *cinéma vérité* mode
of *The Executioner's Song* records the conditions that grant a new
lease on life, as it were, to the American death penalty post-*Gregg*,
provided it can tolerate an undecidable relation between suicide
and the punishment called capital. Once again it is the literary work
that lays these conditions bare, through the example of Gary Gilmore, and bears up under the weight of a truth-telling that has also
to be poetic.

These several relations between death penalty and literature thus
figure the posture of literature or poetry in general before the law
in the latter's most stringent and cruel guise. The configuration is
one that Derrida has described as the mutual condition of literature
coming before the law, which has also to come before literature,
and where "to come before" has both juridical and temporal senses.
That literature comes to stand before the law is quite simply the
condition of what today we call literature, in its modern institution.
Literature thus comes under the protection of the law for its right
to say anything, at least in politico-juridical regimes that would call
themselves democratic. Which is why, as we already read in Chapter
1, Derrida can write in his most sloganistic tone: "No democracy

---

1. See John Stuart Mill, *Public and Parliamentary Speeches, November 1850–November
1868*, ed. by John M. Robson and Bruce L. Kinzer (Toronto: University of Toronto Press,
1988).

without literature; no literature without democracy."[2] The one thus gives the law to the other.

Elsewhere and earlier, in the essay "Before the Law," Derrida works out an extensive analysis of this mutual condition. The essay proposes an expansive reading of Kafka's parable of the same title, in which a man from the country who wants to enter into the law has trouble understanding how the law can be at once singular and universal. That "this gate was made only for you,"[3] as the guardian says to him at the close of the story, had apparently never occurred to him, not surprising given the imposing dimensions of all those powers amassed behind the door before which he stood, and stood, and finally died. The man had failed to see that, by right of the universal law, he had already entered and been accepted, by birth, into the law—he did not have to wait to enter.[4] But Derrida bids us to understand that the trouble for the man of the country stemmed from literature, before the law. For literature is the other name of singular universality/universal singularity:

> There is no literature without work [*œuvre*], without absolutely singular performance, and the *de rigueur* irreplaceability calls up again the questions of the man from the country when the singular crosses the universal, when the categorical engages the idiomatic, as a literature must always do. The man from the country had trouble

2. Jacques Derrida, "Passions: An Oblique Offering," trans. David Wood, in *On the Name*, ed. Thomas Dutoit (Stanford, Calif.: Stanford University Press, 1999), 28.

3. Franz Kafka, "Before the Law," trans. Willa and Edwin Muir, in *The Penal Colony: Stories and Short Pieces* (New York: Schocken, 1948), 150.

4. In a radio interview from 1993, Derrida remarked on the paradox of the law's inaccessibility that Kafka's fable illustrates: "This law . . . is always anterior to any experience of autonomy and it is irreducible to what are called the laws . . . and this law is transcendent, inaccessible, which doesn't mean it is something transcendent, it is myself, in a certain manner, it is I who produce this law. . . . It is because it is I who produce this transcendence that I cannot accede to it and that it is always before me, inaccessible, intangible, even as it addresses me singularly." *L'entretien 03: Jacques Derrida* (Paris: Éditions du sous-sol, 2017) 82; my trans.

understanding the singularity of an access that ought to be universal, which in truth it was. He had trouble with literature.[5]

But what does it mean to have trouble with literature? What does it mean, not just for your average Joe or man-from-the-country, but for the law and for the state, for the state of law, for example (if indeed it is just an example) the law of the death penalty? Does literature, can literature subvert the law, trouble its self-assurance as the law that it claims to be? *Gesetz* (Kafka's title is "Vor dem Gesetz") is also the position, the posing, the setting down (as in writing) of the law, its im-position in an act, which is not just but is also a linguistic act, what we call a performative speech (writing) act. With its necessary performativity, the law once again crosses with the poetic performative of literature in a conjunction that opens up a space of play between them. This space is the possibility of what Derrida calls "a sort of subversive juridicity" of literary works. I quote a long passage from "Before the Law":

> Literature perhaps came to occupy, in historical conditions that
> are not simply linguistic, a place that is always open to a sort of
> subversive juridicity. It would have occupied that place for a certain
> time and without being itself through and through subversive, quite
> to the contrary sometimes. This subversive juridicity supposes that
> self-identity can never be assured or reassuring. It also supposes a
> power to produce performatively utterances of the law, the law that
> can be literature and not only the law to which literature subjects
> itself. It then makes the law, it emerges in that place where the law is
> made. (216)

Derrida then details how, in certain conditions (*dans des conditions déterminées*), literature can use its performative power to get around or even overturn (*tourner*) the existing laws, which all the

---

5. Jacques Derrida, "Before the Law," trans. Avital Ronell, in *Acts of Literature*, ed. Derek Attridge (New York: Routledge, 1992), 213; here and throughout the translation has been modified.

same guarantee it and make it possible for literature to arise. This power to *tourner* the law is literature's own because it is the power of its language to trope and turn in directions or senses that remain finally undecidable, if only by reason of the secrecy that seals the fictional contract. This "referential equivocality" is what allows literature, writes Derrida, to "play the law." "This thanks to the referential equivocality of certain linguistic structures. In these conditions, literature can *play the law*, repeat it by diverting it [*en la détournant*] or by circumventing it [*en la contournant*]" (134). As to these conditions, Derrida specifies them at length.

> These conditions, which are also the conventional conditions of
> any performative, are doubtless not purely linguistic, although
> any convention can in turn give rise to a definition or a contract
> in the order of language. Here we touch upon one of the most
> difficult points to situate, when we have to locate language without
> language, language beyond language, the relations of forces that
> are mute but already haunted by writing, where the conditions of a
> performative, the rules of the game, and the limits of subversion are
> established. (216)

Derrida is reading Kafka's "Before the Law" as just such an instance of the literary work playing the law, but as the foregoing makes clear, he is also seeking to formalize these conditions, at least to the extent allowed by the difficulty of situating, with language, the without or beyond language, where it is a matter of forces and relations of forces. Despite that difficulty, we are given here some coordinates at which to encounter in another work "the ungraspable instant when [literature] plays the law" (216).

Like "Before the Law," Charles Baudelaire's prose poem "Une mort héroïque," "A Heroic Death," is brief and has features of allegory. And like Kafka's story of a man from an unnamed country at an unspecified time, Baudelaire's tale is set in the princely court of *** in some indefinite past. However, rather than continue with para-

phrase, here is a translation of the short text in question. (It is my
own translation not only to avoid issues with copyright but because
I want to rely on a fairly literal version of Baudelaire's language.)[6]

A Heroic Death

Fancioulle was an admirable buffoon, and almost one of the Prince's
friends. But for people destined by their station to the comical,
serious things have fatal attractions, and although it may appear
bizarre that the ideas of fatherland and liberty should despotically
take over the brain of a minstrel, one day Fancioulle joined a
conspiracy formed by several malcontent nobles.

There exist everywhere worthy men ready to denounce to
the powers-that-be those individuals of a black bile humor who
want to overthrow princes and carry out, without consulting it, a
rearrangement of society. The lords in question were arrested, along
with Fancioulle, and destined to a certain death.

I am willing to believe that the Prince was almost angry to find
his favorite player among the rebels. The Prince was neither better
nor worse than any other, but an excessive sensibility made him,
in many cases, more cruel and more despotic than all his peers. A
passionate lover of the fine arts, an excellent connoisseur moreover,
he was really insatiable for voluptuous pleasures. Rather indifferent
in relation to men and morality, a veritable artist himself, he knew no
dangerous enemy except Boredom, and the bizarre efforts he made
to flee or vanquish this tyrant of the world would certainly have
attracted for him, on the part of a severe historian, the epithet of
"monster," if it had been permitted in his domains to write anything
that did not tend uniquely toward pleasure or astonishment, which
is one of the most delicate forms of pleasure. The great misfortune
of this Prince was that he never had a theater vast enough for his
genius. There are young Neros who suffocate within too strict limits,

---

6. There are at present six complete translations in English of *Le spleen de Paris*, also
known as *Petits poèmes en prose*, and several partial translations. I have consulted three of
them: by Aleister Crowley, *Little Poems in Prose* (Chicago: Teitan, 1928); by Louise Varèse,
Paris Spleen (New York: New Directions, 1947); and by Keith Waldrop, *Paris Spleen: Little Poems in Prose* (Middletown, Conn.: Wesleyan University Press, 2009).

and whose names and good intentions will forever be unknown in
the centuries to come. An improvident Providence had given to this
one faculties greater than his estates.

Suddenly the rumor spread that the sovereign wanted to
pardon all the conspirators, and the origin of this rumor was the
announcement of a great spectacle where Fancioulle was supposed
to play one of his principal and best roles, and at which would be
present, people said, even the condemned nobles; an evident sign,
added superficial minds, of the generous tendencies of the offended
Prince.

On the part of such a naturally and willingly eccentric man,
anything was possible, even virtue, even clemency, especially if
he could hope to find unexpected pleasures in it. But for those
who, like myself, had been able to probe deeper into the depths
of this curious, sick soul, it was infinitely more probable that the
Prince wanted to judge the value of the theatrical talents of a man
condemned to death. He wanted to profit from the occasion to do a
physiological experiment of *capital* interest and verify to what extent
the habitual faculties of an artist could be changed or modified by the
extraordinary situation in which he found himself; beyond that, did
there exist in his soul a more or less decided intention of clemency?
It has never been possible to bring this point to light.

Finally, the great day having arrived, this little court deployed all
its pomp, and it would be difficult to conceive, unless one had seen
it, everything that the privileged class of a small state, with limited
resources, can show by way of splendors for a truly solemn occasion.
This one was doubly so, first for the magical luxury displayed, then
for the moral and mysterious interest attaching to it.

Master Fancioulle excelled above all in silent roles or ones with
few words, which are often the principal ones in those fairy-like
dramas whose object is to represent symbolically the mystery of life.
He came on stage lightly and with perfect ease, which helped to
strengthen, in the noble public, the idea of kindness and pardon.

When people say of an actor: "He is a good actor," they are
using a formula that implies that beneath the character one can
still glimpse the actor, that is, the art, the effort, the will. But if an

actor managed to be, relative to the character he is charged with
conveying, what the best statues of antiquity, miraculously come to
life—living, walking, seeing—would be relative to the general and
confused idea of beauty, that would no doubt be a singular case
and altogether unexpected. Fancioulle was, that night, a perfect
idealization, which it was impossible not to suppose living, possible,
real. This buffoon came, went, laughed, wept, convulsed his body,
all the while an invisible halo around his head, invisible halo for
everyone, but visible for me, and in which were mixed together, in
a strange amalgam, the radiance of Art and the glory of Martyrdom.
Fancioulle introduced, through I know not what special grace, the
divine and the supernatural into the most extravagant buffooneries.
My pen trembles and the tears of an always present emotion fill
my eyes when I try to describe for you this unforgettable evening.
Fancioulle proved to me, in a peremptory, irrefutable manner, that
the intoxication of Art is more apt than any other to veil the terrors of
the abyss; that genius can play comedy at the edge of the tomb with a
joy that blocks any view of the tomb, lost, as he is, in a paradise that
excludes all idea of tomb and destruction.

The whole audience, however blasé and frivolous it might be,
soon submitted to the all-powerful domination of the artist. No
one was dreaming any longer of death, mourning, or tortures. All
abandoned themselves, without a worry, to the many voluptuous
pleasures offered by the sight of a living masterpiece of art. Outbursts
of joy and admiration shook the vaults of the edifice several
times with the force of continuous thunder. The Prince, himself,
intoxicated, joined his applause to that of his court.

However, for a clairvoyant eye, his own intoxication was not
without admixture. Did he feel vanquished in his power as despot?
humiliated in his art of terrifying hearts and dulling minds? frustrated
in his hopes and scorned in his expectations? Such suppositions, not
exactly justified although not absolutely unjustifiable, crossed my
mind while I contemplated the Prince's face, on which a new pallor
was being added ceaselessly to his habitual pallor, like snow being
added to snow. His lips were drawn more and more tightly together,

and his eyes were lit by an internal fire similar to that of jealousy and
rancor, even while he was ostensibly applauding the talents of his old
friend, the strange buffoon who was buffooning death so well. At a
certain moment, I saw His Highness lean down toward a little page,
standing just behind him, and speak into his ear. The impish features
of the pretty child lit up with a smile, and then he quickly left the
Prince's loge as if to carry out an urgent commission.

A few minutes later a sharp, prolonged whistle blow interrupted
Fancioulle in one of his best moments, and lacerated both ears
and hearts. And from the place in the room where this unexpected
disapproval had rung out, a child hurried into a corridor while
stifling laughter.

Fancioulle, shaken, awakened from his dream, first closed his
eyes, and when he then opened them again almost right away,
they had grown immeasurably larger, he next opened his mouth as
if to gasp convulsively for breath, staggered forward a little, then
backward a little, and then fell stone dead on the stage.

Had the whistle, swift as a sword, really cheated the executioner?
Had the Prince divined the full homicidal efficacy of his ruse? It
is possible to doubt that. Did he regret his dear and inimitable
Fancioulle? It is sweet and legitimate to believe so.

The guilty nobles had enjoyed for the last time the spectacle of
comedy. The same night they were erased from life.

Since then, several mimes, justly appreciated in various countries,
have come to play before the court of ***, but not one of them was
able to remind people of the wonderful talents of Fancioulle, or rise
to the same *favor*.

Any parallels already mentioned between "A Heroic Death" and
Kafka's parable can now be seen as rather minor when the two
are set side by side. A salient difference is, for example, the former's use of a first-person narrator, the teller of the tale who was
also a witness of the event he recounts (or so goes the fiction) and
through whose voice or rather pen everything passes before passing on to us readers. So one of our questions will doubtless have to

be whether and how this inflection through a particularized narrator affects (or not) literature's scene of playing the law. First, however: Is playing the law indeed the scene being played here and, if so, in what sense?

Fancioulle plays before the law, before the Prince who makes the law and exercises the sovereign right to sentence to death—and to pardon, these being understood as mutually exclusive alternatives, a strict either/or. It is a command performance, and Fancioulle plays for his life. Although the verb "play," "jouer," occurs just three times in the text, it is the essence of the performance, to put it a little redundantly. He performs a play, a role in a play that is specified only as "one of his principal and best roles," a silent role or with few words, a mime rather than a monologue, gestures rather than a spoken part. It is not Hamlet declaiming but more like the players in the play within the play who act out the murder of the old king while playing before the new king.

Playing the law can also refer us to Fancioulle's crime, which is treason against the sovereign. The text's narrator describes the act, however ironically, as driven by the will "to overthrow princes and carry out, without consulting it, a rearrangement of society." Illegitimately, the usurper would play the sovereign and play the law, play the part of society's lawgiver. In this sense, playing the law approaches its most subversive application as well as what Derrida calls "the limits of subversion," where the (unequal) relation of forces can end up enforcing the status quo, as indeed it does here: "The lords in question were arrested, along with Fancioulle, and destined to a certain death [*voués à une mort certaine*]."

It is, then, in the face of this "certain death" that Fancioulle plays. Yet, given that death is always a certainty, the phrase has to be heard bearing the promise or the *vœu* of a certain *kind* of death, the kind that is sovereignly decided in a death sentence. It is a death calculated to be dealt and suffered at a time certain, in execution of the sentence. But the central uncertainty of "A Heroic Death" is precisely whether or not the sovereign calculates the player's death in

the manner of an execution and thereby gets a jump on the headsman, so to speak. The narrator repeatedly dead-ends all such questions in indecisive responses:

> Had the whistle, swift as a sword, really cheated the executioner?
> Had the Prince divined the full homicidal efficacy of his ruse? It
> is possible to doubt that. Did he regret his dear and inimitable
> Fancioulle? It is sweet and legitimate to believe so.

Earlier, a similar question about the Prince's motive in commanding
the spectacle is also suspended in uncertainty: "Did there exist in
his soul a more or less decided intention of clemency? It has never
been possible to bring this point to light [*C'est un point qui n'a
jamais pu être éclairci*]." This latter formula says very precisely the
secret that is always the other's intention, even when it is declared
(for anyone can lie about her intentions).

   Why did the Prince order Fancioulle to perform before the whole
court and his partners in the crime for which he stands condemned,
destined, or promised to a "certain death"? This is the question that
divides the spectators into the two camps of, on the one hand, "superficial minds" and, on the other, those who, like the narrator,
have "been able to probe deeper into the depths of this curious,
sick soul." His informed hypothesis, "infinitely more probable" than
an intention to pardon, is of an experiment meant to test the skills
of an actor condemned to death, which supposes, however, a Prince
not inclined to predetermined outcomes and calculated ends. And
that is consistent with the dominant trait of a despot whose only
enemy is Boredom, that "tyrant of the world." Not knowing the out-
come in advance—the experimenter's stance—gives one the chance
to be surprised, astonished, un-bored. Baudelaire ought to know,
having famously invoked in the dedicatory poem of *Les fleurs du
mal*, "Au lecteur," a monster (the Prince too would be called a monster by the severe historian) who would "willingly make a debris
of the earth / And swallow the world in a yawn." The monster is, of
course, Boredom, *l'Ennui*, and, in the last image of the poem it or he

is described, eyes filled with involuntary tears, dreaming of scaffolds ("*l'oeil chargé d'un pleur involontaire, / Il rêve d'échafauds . . .*").[7]

The Prince, then, will not in all probability have calculated what occurred, either because he is temperamentally adverse to knowing anything with certainty in advance or because he had more or less decided to pardon Fancioulle after his performance. What seems certain, however, is that the performance suspends the actor's sentence of "certain death," executed by the state, in a very uncertain death that in a sense is executed[8] by that other state or *état*, which is the comedian's profession. To see this we have to go back to the second, long sentence of the text, where Fancioulle is first described as fatally destined, that is, *voué*, before being promised, *voué*, to a certain death. He is *voué* or promised by his station, his status, or his state to serious things such as subversion and political treason under the serious guises of fatherland and liberty:

> But for people destined [*voués*, promised, pledged] by their station [*par état*] to the comical, serious things have fatal attractions, and although it may appear bizarre that the ideas of fatherland [*patrie*] and liberty should despotically take over the brain of a minstrel, one day Fancioulle joined a conspiracy formed by several malcontent nobles.

Besides doubling the destiny of his station by the fatality of its attractions, this sentence slips in a hint of the doubling of the sovereign or the despot by Fancioulle, whose mind is said to be "despotically" taken over by ideas of another station and another state, the fatherland. Such doubling is his crime, but it is also his state or station to play (for) the sovereign, to play the law. State against state, one state fatally subverting and playing the other. Fancioulle has bid to subvert the state of the Prince, but the Prince will no less have sought to subvert Fancioulle's state of dramatic illusion.

What happens in Fancioulle's performance? The narrator records

7. Charles Baudelaire, "Au lecteur," in *Œuvres complètes* (Paris: Gallimard, 1975), 1:6.
8. In the sense of *ex+sequi*, to pursue to the end, see Chapter 2.

three versions of the event, three witness accounts or responses. The first account bears witness to the idealized truth and, as such, is attributed to no one in particular or to everyone in general, as the universal truth of the performative event. "Fancioulle was, that night, a perfect idealization, which it was impossible not to suppose living, possible, real." That this was the general reaction to the performance is reiterated when we read that the whole audience "abandoned themselves . . . to the many voluptuous pleasures offered by the sight of a living masterpiece of art." This first account, then, is given in the name of this general or universal public witness.

The second account is the narrator's own singular testimony to what he witnessed that no one else saw, for it was invisible for everyone except him:

> This buffoon came, went, laughed, wept, convulsed his body, all the while an invisible halo around his head, invisible halo for everyone, but visible for me, and in which were mixed together, in a strange amalgam, the radiance of Art and the glory of Martyrdom.

The narrator was thus, in effect, the only witness of a miracle, of something supernatural, saintly, sacred. In the next sentence, the idea of a religious experience is underscored when he claims to see something "divine and supernatural" in Fancioulle's art: "Fancioulle introduced, through I know not what special grace, the divine and the supernatural into the most extravagant buffooneries." This is another "strange amalgam," where the highest idea is mixed with the lowest, and it is not unlike the fatal attraction that draws the comedian by station to serious things, resulting in a mixture that "may appear bizarre." Running through the text is thus a subtle but insistent remarking of bizarre mixtures, strange amalgams, and attraction of opposites. To what effect? We will return to that question.

As witness of a miracle, the narrator will claim to have seen proof of his faith in art:

> Fancioulle proved to me, in a peremptory, irrefutable manner, that
> the intoxication of Art is more apt than any other to veil the terrors of

the abyss; that genius can play comedy at the edge of the tomb with a
joy that blocks any view of the tomb, lost, as he is, in a paradise that
excludes all idea of tomb and destruction.

Here the narrator seems almost to have taken over the position he
supposes to be the Prince's, that of someone testing, as we already
read, "the value of the theatrical talents of a man condemned to
death." Fancioulle, the subject of the experiment, thus gives "peremptory, irrefutable" proof of two things: that he is a talent of genius and that the genius of art blocks any view of death, no matter
how certainly imminent. Notice how this is another claim about
visibility that the narrator is making, although here the claim reverses the poles: It does not claim to see what is invisible to anyone
else, like the halo, but rather *not* to see what in some sense is really
there—certain death. But of course no matter its certainty (and, as
we said, death is always certain), death is never *there* as what can
simply be seen or not seen, visible or invisible. It can seem to be
rendered such only by way of a figure, a trope, which in Baudelaire's text is the metonym *tombe*, tomb, grave. The text lays a curious stress on this figure, using it three times in the space of the final
clause of the passage: "genius can play comedy at the edge of the
tomb with a joy that blocks any view of the **tomb**, lost, as he is, in
a paradise that excludes all idea of **tomb** and destruction." English
translators of Baudelaire's prose poems have shown a reluctance
to follow this odd repetition *à la lettre*. Both Aleister Crowley and
Louise Varèse drop the final *tombe* (in French, one could say they
font tomber la tombe); Keith Waldrop changes the final "grave" to
a plural. It is as if they all suspected Baudelaire of a *faute de style*,
which they wanted to correct.[9] However that may be, the passage
does indeed insist three times, in French, on the word "tombe,"

9. Crowley translates: "at the edge of the tomb . . . prevents it from seeing the tomb . . . all
idea either of death or of destruction" (66); Varèse translates: "on the edge of the grave . . . it
does not see the grave . . . all thought of death and destruction."

which is the very thing (or figure) that the genius of Art is said to veil and to block from view so utterly. An unsettling irony thus afflicts this transfer from the wordless, idealized art of the mime to the wordy and necessarily rhetorical art of the poet, who cannot not name and thus reveal all that Art's genius is supposed to veil. This ironic effect, however, is reserved for the poet's audience of readers, who are thereby reminded again and again of what Fancioulle's public has successfully blocked from its thoughts under "the all-powerful domination of the artist. No one was dreaming any longer of death, mourning, or tortures."

With this all-powerful domination, it is as if Fancioulle had succeeded through his art, at least momentarily, where the plot of political overthrow had failed. The sovereign is no longer sovereign in the people's mind, or at least in the mind of the audience. This is the first thought that occurs to the narrator when, with his "clairvoyant eye" (once again, it is a matter of seeing what others cannot), he notices that the Prince's intoxication with the performance is not "without admixture," that is, *sans mélange*. And he wonders: "Did he feel vanquished in his power as despot?" Here, then, is the third version of Fancioulle's performance, as reflected in the face of the Prince who watches it through eyes that, according to the narrator, are "lit by an internal fire similar to that of jealousy and rancor." The narrator can imagine several possible reasons for the apparent displeasure of the sovereign:

> Did he feel vanquished in his power as despot? humiliated in his art
> of terrifying hearts and dulling minds? frustrated in his hopes and
> scorned in his expectations? Such suppositions, not exactly justified
> although not absolutely unjustifiable, crossed my mind while I
> contemplated the Prince's face . . .

Consistent with his refusal to pronounce on the Prince's motives and calculations, the narrator makes only plausible suppositions for his apparent ill temper: the performance had overthrown his own power; the performance had shown up his "art" of terror with the

counterterror of an art that veils the threat of death; the performance had dashed his hopes to see Fancioulle fail to conquer the
fear of his certain death, and instead the experiment yielded proof
of the Prince's own powerlessness. These suppositions are in fact
variations of the same insight into the Prince's decision to interrupt
the performance via the page's prank and then see what happens.

What happens, it seems, is astonishing.

> Fancioulle, shaken, awakened from his dream, first closed his eyes,
> and when he then opened them again almost right away, they had
> grown immeasurably larger, he next opened his mouth as if to gasp
> convulsively for breath, staggered forward a little, then backward a
> little, and then fell stone dead on the stage [*tomba roide mort sur*
> *les planches*].

Astonishment, the narrator has earlier remarked, "is one of the
most delicate forms of pleasure," and the Prince appears to have
procured this pleasure by executing Fancioulle without executing
him and without calculating his death. "Had the whistle, swift as a
sword, really cheated the executioner? Had the Prince divined the
full homicidal efficacy of his ruse? It is possible to doubt that." Not
an execution, then, yet a "certain death" inflicted by the sovereign,
pursuant to a death sentence. Once again, however, it is the notion
of "a certain death" that hangs suspended from the uncertainties
and doubts that the narrator floats over the scene.

But the narrator's doubts are not the only ones that could be
formulated. A "certain death" means also a verified death, one that
has been attested and thus made certain. We are told that Fancioulle
"fell stone dead on the stage," but this cliché—in addition to filling
in the void of the figurative *tombe* with the literal action of falling,
that is, *tomber*—alerts one to the seeming staginess of the death
throes that Fancioulle undergoes, as if he were acting them out with
his consummate art that "it was impossible not to suppose living,
possible, real" or, rather, at this end of his performance, that it was
impossible not to suppose dead, really dead, and not merely "sur les

planches," on the stage. No doubt it is a scene the actor has played
many times, when he had to mime a character's death. Beyond its
description of the actor's last stagey gestures, Baudelaire's text says
nothing to suggest that Fancioulle's certain death was merely acted,
that he played dead. That silence, however, also contradicts nothing and leaves open the possibility that Fancioulle had just played
at dying and death.

Another doubt may be entertained. If Fancioulle really died that
day, if his death was certain and certified, then was it not just a "heroic death," as the title has it, one that achieves the "glory of Martyrdom" (indeed a double martyrdom—for a political cause and for
the religion of Art), but a merciful death, or even a *grâce*, that is, a
pardon? Recall that whether or not the Prince harbored the intention to pardon Fancioulle is the point that "it has not been possible
to bring to light," not even for the clairvoyant narrator. The secret
of grace or pardon hovers over the performance for the spectators,
it fuels the "moral and mysterious interest attaching to [the occa-
sion]," but it also qualifies Fancioulle's playing that "introduced,
through *I know not what special grace*, the divine and the supernatural into the most extravagant buffooneries" (emphasis added).
The secret of Fancioulle's grace and the secret of the Prince's intention to *grâcier* or pardon (or not) seem to communicate in the text
at a level where it is precisely not a question of anyone's intention,
including Baudelaire's. By this I mean that "A Heroic Death" can
be read as operating on a plane where opposites attract without
canceling each other out, where the Prince and the Fool are equally
sovereign and therefore neither is sovereign, where the *grâce* or
pardon of the one has perhaps been preempted by the poetic grace
of the other, and where a death penalty can be delivered or received
as a pardon, a grace, an *arrêt de mort*, as one can say in French.

It is on this plane of radical irony that I would situate the singular performance of Baudelaire's text, its "*de rigueur* irreplaceabil-
ity," as Derrida calls it, in the letter of its law. But irony is doubtless not the right term here, especially in the vicinity of Baudelaire,

who, so say many, can almost always be read as ironic. No doubt
the use of italics on two words in "A Heroic Death" signals such
an ironic intention,[10] and thus one should understand an at least
double sense for both "capital" ("of a *capital* interest") and "favor,"
the text's italicized final word. The italics serve as arched eyebrows
or scare-quote fingers to the address of the reader, getting her attention. But I have in mind an "irony," to keep the name, that affects even such apparent ironic intentions, be it Baudelaire's, the
narrator's, or the Prince's. It can suspend or even cancel intentional
irony with a kind of impossible truth that only the singular performance of the poetic work can sustain. In "A Heroic Death," that impossible truth declares itself in a pardon by execution—or an execution by pardon, for it is the same reversibility. Whether or not the
Prince intended to pardon him, Fancioulle dies, executed, in a state
of grace. It is thus an execution graced with a pardon, as if the *arrêt
de mort*, the death sentence, were also an *arrêt de mort*, a pardon,
a reprieve, in an undecidable arrest, or restless hesitation, between
the two movements, one promising a certain death and the other
suspending, deferring, delaying, arresting the first movement.[11]

Perhaps, then, the text of this singular performance plays the
law? We have tested many possible senses of that phrase, but at least
one is outstanding: to play the law in the sense of duping it, fooling
it, or outplaying it. The Prince would have been outplayed, fooled
into pardoning his fool in the very act that also punishes treachery.
But if so, how is that the *doing* of a text that purports merely to
recount the event? Such a question supposes that said event would
have taken place somewhere *outside* the singular performance of

10. Claude Pichois, the editor of the Pléiade edition of *Le spleen de Paris*, notes that these
italics conform to Baudelaire's habit of picking out "familiar anecdotes, familiar allusions, familiar expressions" for their prosaic worth; Baudelaire, *Œuvres complètes*, 1:1302.

11. On the equivocal possibilities of this phrase, see Jacques Derrida, "Living On," trans.
James Hulbert, in *Parages*, ed. John P. Leavey (Stanford, Calif.: Stanford University Press, 2011),
which is in part a commentary on the text by Maurice Blanchot *L'arrêt de mort* (Paris: Gallimard, 1948).

the text. It supposes, that is, a stable referential regime rather than a performative regime, in which "truth" is made—and played. Such a supposed referential regime is also the fiction that the text projects and maintains, over against the fact, which is the fact of the fiction, that *there is no outside-the-text*, that it exercises what Derrida has called reference without referent.[12] That essential condition of fiction, in effect even when one detects reference to a context "in the real," puts one under the obligation to credit its performance without believing it. And that is the attitude required of readers of "A Heroic Death" so that it can perform a truth beyond belief, according to which a princely pardon may be enacted as execution of a death sentence for a capital crime.

I have suggested that this performance plays the law in several senses. Another sense to consider is its relation to a law of censorship like the one that the text mentions in passing when filling in its portrait of the Prince's cruelty: Surely, says our narrator, a historian would have called him a monster, "if it had been permitted in his domains to write anything that did not tend exclusively toward pleasure or astonishment." "Une mort héroïque" was first published in 1863, six years after the conviction of *Les fleurs du mal*, the poet, and his publisher for "outrage against public morality," which is the same year that *Madame Bovary*, its author, and its publisher were likewise put on trial for the same offense. It is possible to read the text of "A Heroic Death" as turning aside or "playing" this censor with tried and true techniques of allegory: A nameless Prince in the place of the self-styled emperor Napoléon III, a court of *** (those asterisks alone signal allegory) in the place of this emperor's illegitimately installed government, and the comedian, mime, or actor

---

12. "The act plays out a difference without reference, or rather without a referent, without any absolute exteriority, and hence without any inside." Jacques Derrida, "The Double Session," in *Dissemination*, trans. Barbara Johnson (Chicago: University of Chicago Press, 1981), 219. In question is the mime performance of "Pierrot Murderer of His Wife," as evoked by Mallarmé's prose poem "Mimique," a text whose premise of a mimed death might itself evoke "Une mort héroïque."

Fancioulle in the place, well, in the place of the Artist in general, unless it is the subversive revolutionary in general—or even in particular. It has been suggested, not implausibly, that Fancioulle's last act evokes the execution of Felice Orsini, the Italian revolutionary and leader of the *Carbonari*, who made a bloody assassination attempt against Napoléon III in January 1858, for which crime he was condemned and guillotined two months later.[13] The name "Fancioulle" certainly calls up the Italian *fanciullo*, boy or child, as well as the Italian tradition of theatrical mime and mask in the *commedia dell'arte*.[14] "A Heroic Death" would thus salute, under the radar of censorship, the Italian bomb thrower. But it has just as plausibly been suggested that the player evokes the original dandy, George "Beau" Brummell, who lost the favor of the Prince Regent and had to exile himself to France to escape his creditors.[15]

To be sure, such striking historical tableaux enrich the apprehension of a poetic work that, as Walter Benjamin showed so firmly, is itself thoroughly historical in the most essential sense.[16] They cannot displace the fact, however, that apprehension of a fiction like "A Heroic Death" is never certain, unlike certain death. Indeed, this fundamental or structural uncertainty is the condition of a work's surviving beyond the memory of anyone's death, beginning with the poet's or the author's, but also the deaths of Orsini, Brummell, Napoléon III, George IV, and so forth. Baudelaire's prose poem, like each of the other works taken up in this book, suspends the certainty and calculation of the death penalty from this structure of

13. For this association, see Peter Schofer, "'Une mort héroïque': Baudelaire's Social Theater of Cruelty," in Theater and Society in French Literature, *French Literature Series 15* (1988), 50–57.

14. Crowley restores this Italian context by rendering Fancioulle's name as Fanciullo.

15. See Claire Nicolay, "The 'Fatal Attractions' of 'Serious Things': Regency Politics and Performance in Baudelaire's *Le Spleen de Paris*," *European Romantic Review* 11, no. 3 (2008): 322–347.

16. See Walter Benjamin, *Charles Baudelaire: Un poète lyrique à l'apogée du capitalisme*, trans. Jean Lacoste (Paris: Petite Bibliothèque Payot, 1982).

fiction's uncertainty, its mode of reference without referent, which is in force even when historically real persons, like the Rosenbergs or Gary Gilmore, are put in play in the fiction's fabric.

As for the incalculable millions and millions of others executed throughout the history of the world, they still wait for the story to be told.[17]

17. A remarkable blog has made a small dent on this deficit. Edited anonymously by one who calls himself "The Headsman," *Executed Today* has for the last ten years posted every day "the story of an historical execution that took place on this date, and the story behind it"; see http://www.executedtoday.com/about/.

POSTMORTEM

For a long time I have been worrying about how to conclude this book. Like Mailer, I seemed to have become "bad at endings." Just as an index of how bad it was, the last sentence of Chapter 5 took me two days to find, which is not to say it was necessarily worth the wait. Perhaps a long vigil by the side of gallows or guillotines, electric chairs or gas chambers has to end up making one eager to delay the final execution and leery of the "Finis" that, for Benjamin, signals the "limit at which [the novelist] invites the reader to a divinatory realization of the meaning of life."[18] This is not a novel, of course, but given its preoccupation with novels and other fictions, maybe something like that limit has made an impression on it.

Hence the idea of skipping past the end to a sort of *postmortem*.

It so happens that the four principal literary works considered here all extend their narratives past the executed end (by hanging, by electric chair, by firing squad, or by a whistle that "lacerated both ears and hearts"). In Orwell's story, the hanging party goes off hilariously to toast its success while the executed man still hung not a hundred yards distant. *A Public Burning* ends with an "Epilogue" where poor Richard Nixon has to be sodomized by Uncle Sam before he can embody the spirit of the nation. And Fancioulle's

---

18. Walter Benjamin, "The Storyteller: Observations on the Work of Nikolai Leskov," trans. Harry Zohn, in *Selected Writings*, vol. 3, ed. Michael W. Jennings (Cambridge, Mass.: The Belknap Press of Harvard University Press, 2002), 155.

death performance is succeeded by all the other jesters who came to
the court of *** without being able to rival him in public memory.

As for *The Executioner's Song*, its extension past the end includes
a long report *postmortem* in the clinical sense of the term. It is
near the end of the book, in a chapter titled "The Remains." The
three-and-a-half-page detailed description of the autopsy is narrated
dispassionately, like the rest of the novel, from a witness's account.
First a team removed organs for donation, and specifically the eyes,
for which Gary himself had chosen the recipient. The executed
man's body was then disemboweled; next its brain was removed, after its face had been pulled down "and was inside out like the back
of a rubber mask."[19] When it was extracted, the heart was so pulver-
ized it was unrecognizable as a heart. The operation concluded by
putting the remaining organs back in the corpse, refitting the top
of the skull, pulling the face back right side out, and sewing everything up.

But the *postmortem* narration does not end there. The same witness accompanies Gary's body to a crematorium. Soon after the
casket with Gary's body had been pushed into the oven, a door was
opened, and the witness "could see Gary's head. Already the scalp
was burning and the skin was falling off to the side." The account
continues:

> Scott could see Gary's face going, and the top flesh blacken and
> disappear. Then the muscle began to burn, and Gilmore's arms which
> had been folded on his chest came up from the tightening, and lifted
> until the fingers of both hands were pointing at the sky. That was the
> very last recognition Jerry Scott had of him. (*ES*, 1047–1048)

The narrative next follows the ashes from the crematorium until
they are finally scattered from an airplane over Provo, Utah, and
environs.

---

19. Norman Mailer, *The Executioner's Song* (New York: Little, Brown, 1979), 1046; hereafter *ES*.

These extensions of the narrative beyond the end that is a death penalty can be easily accounted for as the condition of a witness who must also be a survivor, like Orwell's narrator or Baudelaire's. This condition is not met with in fictions like Camus's *The Stranger* or Wright's *Native Son*, both of which, you may recall, end with the condemned man's anticipation of his imminent end. Neither Meursault's nor Bigger Thomas's death has a diegetic witness, and no one in either narrative ever sees them die and survives to tell about it. Yet this distinction is superficial and finally not a distinction at all when literature's own structure as surviving is taken into account, its living-on as mode of life without what is called life or beyond it. After it, after the end, *postmortem*. Thus Meursault's witness survives as a text as does Bigger's, although in the latter case it is also amply supplemented by a pervasive, even intrusive narrator who constantly makes up for the lag in Bigger's own conscious realizations.[20] Whether or not it is diegetically represented, then, surviving remains the structure of all these works. Surviving remains: These are also ashes.

Finally, I want to acknowledge that, however ashen, melancholic, or mournful, these literary survivals have ambiguous, even ambivalent relations to the death penalty that they variously represent. On the one hand, you could say they *live on* or *live off* (the two can mean the same thing) the death penalty, as a historical and actual practice. For the role of the witness, as we have seen, also fulfills the law of the death penalty; it supplements and completes it: no death penalty, in the strict and modern legal sense, without a third-party witness. There is thus an always possible collusion, reinforcement, or enabling of the law by the singular witness of literature. One

---

20. Abdul JanMohamed, in his study of the novel, makes little distinction, finally, between the narrator's and the character's awareness "in the gradual coming to consciousness of the dialectic of death." Abdul R. JanMohamed, *The Death-Bound Subject: Richard Wright's Archaeology of Death* (Durham, NC: Duke University Press, 2005), 108. "At times," he remarks, "the border between Bigger and the narrator totally disappears" (79).

troubling, albeit virtual version of this collusion or enabling is the claim in "A Heroic Death" that "the intoxication of Art is more apt than any other to veil the terrors of the abyss." With this affirmation, made on the strength of "peremptory, irrefutable" proof, Baudelaire's narrator might well be touting virtues of the best, "most apt" anesthetic to correctional authorities in search of an anesthetic, an "intoxication," to replace all the drugs that have been denied to them, or proven ineffective, or discontinued for use in lethal injections where chemically "veil[ing] the terrors of the abyss" is finally what is required. Art as anesthetic, at once aesthetic and anesthetic, is the very thing, might think these authorities, with which to please everyone (after all, it's Art!) and rescue the remnant of capital punishment in the United States from its slow and painful death without anesthesia. So, again on the one hand, there is art or Art (which includes the literature of a modernity that Baudelaire helped invent) as reanesthetization and reenabling of the death penalty. You just have to imagine a new lethal injection protocol that begins with a dose of Art™ (patent pending).

On the other hand, however, one could say that, in relation to the death penalties they represent, these literary survivals *live on* or *outlive* them in the sense of living more, not just longer but also more intensely, diffusely, or profusely—virtually without end. In this regard, they are the ashes or remains of a phantasm that would calculate the end, know death as "a certain death," as the end and execution of a sentence that leaves no remainder, no grey area where the division and difference of life from death is not decidable by the cut of a decision. In literature, this undecidability, which remains the condition of all decision, survives the phantasm. The radical ambiguity and absolute secret of fiction shelters it, guards it, but also disseminates it, scatters it without end. Remaining to be gathered up, for a time, in endless acts of reading.

ACKNOWLEDGMENTS

This book benefited from many discussions with colleagues and students over the past several years. Students in the graduate seminar "Literature and the Death Penalty" at the University of Southern California in 2014, who were the initial interlocutors for much of my thinking on the subject, gave me many more things, and texts, to think about. Kas Saghafi's invitation to the Spindel Conference at the University of Memphis provided the opportunity to reflect out loud on implications of the death penalty seminar with a number of foremost Derrida scholars. Another such opportunity was the DePaul Humanities Conference in 2013 organized by Elizabeth Rottenberg, who has been unstinting in her advice and help on this project since the beginning. I thank Michael Naas for his invitation to the Collegium Phænomenologicum in 2015 to lecture on the first volume of Derrida's death penalty seminar, which offered the occasion for intense exchanges with a remarkable group of young scholars. Willy Thayer, Elizabeth Collingwood-Selby, and their colleagues and students at the Universidad Metropolitana de Ciencias de la Educación in Santiago, Chile, were generous and genial hosts when I presented three of the book's chapters there in 2016. And César Pérez Sánchez was a patient guide to the city during my stay. I thank Nicholas Royle for his invitation to the University of Sussex to present one of the book's chapters and for our long conversations in Seaford. I also want to thank Hilary Schor, Nomi Stolzenberg, and Ariela Gross for the invitation to present work from the book at the Center for Law, History, and Culture at USC. Thanks, too, to my good friend Mitchell Greenberg, chair of the Department of Romance Studies at Cornell University, for arranging for me to give a talk from the book. Most recently, it was my good fortune to return to DePaul University at the invitation of its Department of Philosophy to present work from the book: I thank Peg Birmingham, Pascale-Anne Brault, Michael Naas, and Elizabeth Rottenberg for their warm welcome and infinite conversation.

For the gift of his friendship and his example as a translator of Derrida's *Death Penalty* seminar, I thank Silvano Facioni.

Katy LeBris provided research help at an early stage of this project and Sam Solomon at an even earlier stage. The two readers for Fordham University Press were each very thoughtful and helpful in their comments, for which I thank them. I am also grateful to Jacques Lezra for his response to the project and for bringing it to Tom Lay, whose forthright editorial advice has no doubt made this a better book than it might have been.

The Derrida Seminars Translation Project workshop has supplied me with a week's annual intellectual stimulation, more than enough to keep me going the rest of the year. For the intensity and honesty of this collaboration over the last ten years, I have many to thank: Elizabeth, Michael, and Pascale-Anne (again, again, and again), Geoff Bennington and David Wills, as well as Ellen Burt, Katie Chenoweth, and Kir Kuiken, not to mention (at least not by name; you know who you are) all the graduate students who took part over the years in our dogged quest for a still better translation.

An earlier version of chapter 1 appeared in *Deconstructing the Death Penalty: Derrida's Seminars and the New Abolitionism*, ed. Kelly Oliver and Stephanie M. Straub, Fordham University Press, 2018.

BIBLIOGRAPHY

Adelsberg, Geoffrey, Lisa Guenther, and Scott Zeman. *Death and Other Penalties: Philosophy in a Time of Mass Incarceration*. New York: Fordham University Press, 2015.

Alexander, Michelle. *The New Jim Crow: Mass Incarceration in the Age of Colorblindness*. Rev. ed. New York: The New Press, 2012.

Althouse, Ann. "Standing, in Fluffy Slippers." *Virginia Law Review* 77, no. 6 (September 1991): 1177–1200.

Anderson, Benedict. *Imagined Communities: Reflections on the Origins and Spread of Nationalism*. 3rd ed. London: Verso, 2006.

Badinter, Robert. *L'abolition*. Paris: Librairie Arthème Fayard, 2000.

———. *L'exécution*. Paris: Grasset, 1973.

Baldwin, James. *Nobody Knows My Name*. New York: Vintage, 1961.

———. *Notes of a Native Son*. Boston: Beacon, 1984.

Banner, Stuart. *The Death Penalty: An American Institution*. Cambridge, Mass.: Harvard University Press, 2003.

Barbour, Charles. *Derrida's Secret: Perjury, Testimony, Oath*. Edinburgh: Edinburgh University Press, 2017.

Barton, John Cyril. *Literary Executions: Capital Punishment and American Culture*. Baltimore, Md.: Johns Hopkins University Press, 2014.

Baudelaire, Charles. *Little Poems in Prose*. Trans. Aleister Crowley. Chicago: Teitan, 1928.

———. *Œuvres complètes I*. Ed. Claude Pichois. Paris: Gallimard, 1975.

———. *Paris Spleen*. Trans. Louise Varèse. New York: New Directions, 1947.

———. *Paris Spleen: Little Poems in Prose*. Trans. Keith Waldrop. Middletown, Conn.: Wesleyan University Press, 2009.

Beccaria, Cesare. *On Crimes and Punishments*. 5th ed. Trans. Graeme R.
Newman and Pietro Marongiu. New Brunswick, N.J.: Transaction,
2009.

Benjamin, Walter. *Charles Baudelaire: Un poète lyrique à l'apogée du
capitalisme*. Trans. Jean Lacoste. Paris: Petite Bibliothèque Payot,
1982.

———. "The Storyteller: Observations on the Work of Nikolai Leskov." In
Selected Writings, ed. Michael W. Jennings, trans. Harry Zohn, 3:143–
166. Cambridge, Mass.: The Belknap Press of Harvard University
Press, 2002.

Bennington, Geoffrey. "Ex Lex." *Oxford Literary Review* 35, no. 2
(2013): 143–163.

———. "Rigor: Or Stupid Uselessness." *Southern Journal of Philosophy*
50, Spindel Supplement (2012): 20–38.

Berger, Eric. "Lethal Injection Secrecy and Eighth Amendment Due Process." *Boston College Law Review* 55 (2014): 1367–1441.

Blanchot, Maurice. *The Work of Fire*. Trans. Charlotte Mandell. Stanford,
Calif.: Stanford University Press, 1995.

Bowers, William, et al. *Legal Homicide: Death as Punishment in America, 1864–1982*. Boston: Northeastern University Press, 1984.

Brooks, Peter. *Reading for the Plot: Design and Intention in Narrative*.
New York: Knopf, 1984.

Brown, Michelle. *The Culture of Punishment: Prison, Society, and Spectacle*. New York: New York University Press, 2009.

Burt, E. S. "The Autobiographical Subject and the Death Penalty." *Oxford
Literary Review* 35, no. 2 (2013): 165–187.

———. "Listening for a Man Swinging: Witnessing in 'The Ballad of Reading Gaol.'" In *Death Sentences: Literature and State Killing*, ed.
B. Christ and È. Morisi. Oxford: Legenda, forthcoming.

Camus, Albert. *L'étranger*. Paris: Gallimard, 1942.

———. *The Stranger*. Trans. Matthew Ward. New York: Knopf, 1988.

Canuel, Mark. *The Shadow of Death: Literature, Romanticism, and the
Subject of Punishment*. Princeton, N.J.: Princeton University Press,
2007.

Coover, Robert. *The Brunist Day of Wrath*. Ann Arbor: Dzanc, 2014.

———. "On *The Public Burning*." *Flashpoint*. http://www.flashpointmag
.com/cooverpubburn.htm.

———. *The Origin of the Brunists*. New York: G. P. Putnam's Sons, 1966.

———. *The Public Burning*. New York: Viking, 1977.

———. "*The Public Burning* Log, 1966–77." *Critique: Studies in Contemporary Fiction* 42, no. 1 (2000): 84–114.

———. "Tears of a Clown." *Critique: Studies in Contemporary Fiction* 42, no. 1 (2000): 1–3.

Cope, Jackson. *Robert Coover's Fictions*. Baltimore, Md.: Johns Hopkins University Press, 1986.

Craven, Alice Mikal, and William E. Dow, eds. *Richard Wright in a Post-Racial Imaginary*. London: Bloomsbury, 2014.

Culbert, Jennifer L. *Dead Certainty: The Death Penalty and the Problem of Judgment*. Stanford, Calif.: Stanford University Press, 2008.

Daoud, Kamel. *Meursault, contre-enquête*. Arles: Actes Sud, 2014.

———. *The Meursault Investigation*. Trans. John Cullen. New York: Other Press, 2015.

Death Penalty Information Center. http://www.deathpenaltyinfo.org/documents/FactSheet.pdf.

DeathPenaltyUSA. http://deathpenaltyusa.org.htm.

Derrida, Jacques. *Acts of Literature*. Ed. Derek Attridge. New York: Routledge, 1992.

———. *Acts of Religion*. Ed. Gil Anidjar. New York: Routledge, 2002.

———. "Cinema and Its Ghosts: An Interview." Trans. Peggy Kamuf. *Discourse* 37, nos. 1/2 (Winter/Spring 2015): 22–39.

———. *The Death Penalty, Volume I*. Ed. Geoffrey Bennington, Marc Crépon, and Thomas Dutoit. Trans. Peggy Kamuf. Chicago: University of Chicago Press, 2013.

———. *The Death Penalty, Volume II*. Ed. Geoffrey Bennington and Marc Crépon. Trans. Elizabeth Rottenberg. Chicago: University of Chicago Press, 2017.

———. *Demeure: Fiction and Testimony*. Trans. Elizabeth Rottenberg. Stanford, Calif.: Stanford University Press, 2000.

———. *Dissemination*. Trans. Barbara Johnson. Chicago: University of Chicago Press, 1981.

———. *Given Time, I: Counterfeit Money*. Trans. Peggy Kamuf. Chicago: University of Chicago Press, 1992.

———. *On the Name.* Ed. Thomas Dutoit. Stanford, Calif.: Stanford University Press, 1999.

———. *The Politics of Friendship.* Trans. George Collins. London: Verso, 1997.

———. *Parages.* Ed. John P. Leavey. Trans. Tom Conley et al. Stanford, Calif.: Stanford University Press, 2011.

———. *Psyche: Inventions of the Other.* Vol. 1. Ed. Peggy Kamuf and Elizabeth Rottenberg. Stanford, Calif.: Stanford University Press, 2007.

———. *Rogues: Two Essays on Reason.* Trans. Pascale-Anne Brault and Michael Naas. Stanford, Calif.: Stanford University Press, 2005.

———. *Séminaire, La peine de mort, Volume I (1999–2000).* Ed. Geoffrey Bennington, Marc Crépon, and Thomas Dutoit. Paris: Éditions Galilée, 2012.

———. *Séminaire, La peine de mort, Volume II (2000–2001).* Ed. Geoffrey Bennington, Marc Crépon, and Thomas Dutoit. Paris: Éditions Galilée, 2015.

———. *The Truth in Painting.* Trans. Geoffrey Bennington and Ian McLeod. Chicago: University of Chicago Press, 1987.

Derrida, Jacques, and Elisabeth Roudinesco. *For What Tomorrow: A Dialogue.* Trans. Jeff Fort. Stanford, Calif.: Stanford University Press, 2004.

Detweiler, Robert. *Uncivil Rites: American Fiction, Religion, and the Public Sphere.* Urbana: University of Illinois Press, 1996.

Didion, Joan. "'I Want to Go Ahead and Do It.'" *New York Times Book Review*, October 7, 1979. http://www.nytimes.com/books/97/05/04/reviews/mailer-song.html.

Dilts, Andrew. "Death Penalty 'Abolition' in Neoliberal Times: The SAFE California Act and the Nexus of Savings and Security." In *Death and Other Penalties: Philosophy in a Time of Mass Incarceration*, ed. G. Adelsberg et al. New York: Fordham University Press, 2015.

Doctorow, E. L. *The Book of Daniel.* New York: Random House, 1971.

Edmundson, Mark. "Romantic Self-Creations: Mailer and Gilmore in *The Executioner's Song.*" *Contemporary Literature* 31, no. 4 (Winter 1990): 434–447.

L'entretien 03: Jacques Derrida. Paris: Éditions du sous-sol, 2017.

Evenson, Brian. *Understanding Robert Coover.* Columbia: University of South Carolina Press, 2003.

Executed Today. http://www.executedtoday.com.

Foucault, Michel. *Discipline and Punish: The Birth of the Prison.* Trans. Alan Sheridan. New York: Vintage, 1977.

Friedland, Paul. *Seeing Justice Done: The Age of Spectacular Capital Punishment in France.* Oxford: Oxford University Press, 2012.

Fritsch, Matthias. "Derrida on the Death Penalty." *Southern Journal of Philosophy 50*, Spindel Supplement (2012): 56–73.

Fulton, Gwynne. "'Phantasmatics': Sovereignty and the Image of Death in Derrida's Death Penalty Seminars." *Mosaic* 48, no. 3 (September 2015): 75–94.

Garland, David. *Peculiar Institution: America's Death Penalty in an Age of Abolition.* Cambridge, Mass.: The Belknap Press of Harvard University Press, 2010.

Gopnik, Adam. "The Caging of America." *New Yorker*, January 30, 2012. http://www.newyorker.com/magazine/2012/01/30/the-caging-of-america.

Guest, David. *Sentenced to Death: The American Novel and Capital Punishment.* Oxford: University Press of Mississippi, 1997.

Hugo, Victor. *Le dernier jour d'un condamné.* In *Œuvres complètes*, vol. 19, Roman II. Paris: J. Hetzel and A. Quentin, 1881.

———. *Écrits sur la peine de mort.* Arles: Actes Sud, 1979.

JanMohamed, Abdul R. *The Death-Bound Subject: Richard Wright's Archaeology of Death.* Durham, N.C.: Duke University Press, 2005.

Justice Policy Institute. http://www.justicepolicy.org/uploads/justicepolicy/documents/jpi_poster.

Kafka, Franz. *The Penal Colony: Stories and Short Pieces.* Trans. Willa Muir and Edwin Muir. New York: Schocken, 1948.

Kamuf, Peggy. "At the Heart of the Death Penalty." *Oxford Literary Review* 35, no. 2 (2013): 24–51.

———. *Book of Addresses.* Stanford, Calif.: Stanford University Press, 2005.

———. "Protocol: Death Penalty Addiction." *Southern Journal of Philosophy 50*, Spindel Supplement (2012): 5–19.

———. *To Follow: The Wake of Jacques Derrida.* Edinburgh: Edinburgh University Press, 2010.

Kant, Immanuel. *The Metaphysics of Morals.* Ed. and trans. Mary Gregor. Cambridge: Cambridge University Press, 1996.

Kaplan, Alice. *Looking for the Stranger: Albert Camus and the Life of a Literary Classic*. Chicago: University of Chicago Press, 2016.

——. "*Meursault, contre-enquête* de Kamel Daoud." *Contreligne*, June 2014. http://www.contreligne.eu/2014/06/kamel-daoud-meursault -contre-enquete/.

Kermode, Frank. *The Sense of an Ending: Studies in the Theory of Fiction*. Oxford: Oxford University Press, 1966.

King, Stephen. *The Green Mile: The Complete Serial Novel*. New York: Pocket, 1996.

Koestler, Arthur, and Albert Camus. *Réflexions sur la peine capitale*. Paris: Gallimard, 2007.

Laplanche, Jean, and J.-B. Pontalis. *Vocabulaire de la psychanalyse*. Paris: PUF, 1967.

Mailer, Norman. *Cannibals and Christians*. New York: Dial, 1966.

——. *The Executioner's Song*. New York: Little, Brown, 1979.

——. *The Presidential Papers*. New York: G. P. Putnam's Sons, 1963.

——. *The Prisoner of Sex*. New York: Little, Brown, 1971.

——. *The White Negro*. San Francisco: City Lights, 1970.

Malley, Timothy. *The Covert Sphere: Secrecy, Fiction, and the National Security State*. Ithaca, N.Y.: Cornell University Press, 2012.

McCaffery, Larry. "As Guilty as the Rest of Them: An Interview with Robert Coover." *Critique: Studies in Contemporary Fiction* 42, no. 1 (2000): 115–125.

Merrill, Robert. "Mailer's Sad Comedy: *The Executioner's Song*." *Texas Studies in Literature and Language* 34, no. 1 (Spring 1992): 129–148.

Michaud, Ginette. *Tenir au secret (Derrida, Blanchot)*. Paris: Éditions Galilée, 2006.

Mill, John Stuart. *Public and Parliamentary Speeches, November 1850–November 1868*. Ed. John M. Robson and Bruce L. Kinzer. Toronto: University of Toronto Press, 1988.

Millett, Kate. *Sexual Politics*. Garden City, N.Y.: Doubleday, 1970.

Naas, Michael. "*Comme si, comme ça*: Following Derrida on the Phantasms of the Self, the State, and a Sovereign God." In *Derrida from Now On*. New York: Fordham University Press, 2008.

——. "The Philosophy and Literature of the Death Penalty: Two Sides of the Same Sovereign." *Southern Journal of Philosophy 50*, Spindel Supplement (2012): 39–55.

Nabokov, Vladimir. "On Translating *Eugene Onegin*." *New Yorker*, January 8, 1955.

Nicolay, Claire. "The 'Fatal Attractions' of 'Serious Things': Regency Politics and Performance in Baudelaire's *Le Spleen de Paris*." *European Romantic Review* 11, no. 3 (2008): 322–347.

Nietzsche, Friedrich. *On the Genealogy of Morals*. Trans. Walter Kaufmann and R. J. Hollingdale. New York: Vintage, 1989.

Norman, Barnaby. "Time of Death: Derrida/Herzog." *Oxford Literary Review* 35, no. 2 (2013): 205–220.

Ogletree, Charles J. Jr., and Austin Sarat, ed. *Life without Parole: America's New Death Penalty?* New York: NYU Press, 2012.

Orwell, George. "As I Please." *Tribune*, November 3, 1944. http://www.telelib.com/words/authors/O/OrwellGeorge/essay/tribune/index.html.

———. *Burmese Days*. New York: Harcourt, 1934.

———. *Facing Unpleasant Facts: Narrative Essays*. Ed. George Packer. New York: Houghton Mifflin Harcourt, 2008.

Oshinsky, David. *Capital Punishment on Trial: "Furman v. Georgia" and the Death Penalty in Modern America*. Lawrence: University of Kansas Press, 2010.

Peterson, Christopher. *Bestial Traces: Race, Sexuality, Animality*. New York: Fordham University Press, 2013.

Potter, Harry. *Hanging in Judgement: Religion and the Death Penalty in England from the Bloody Code to Abolition*. London: SCM, 1993.

Prosperi, Adriano. *Delitto e perdono: La pena di morte nell'orizzonte mental dell'Europa cristiana, XIV–XVIII secolo*. Turin: Giulio Einaudi, 2013.

Rollyson, Carl E. Jr. "Biography in a New Key." *Chicago Review* 31, no. 4 (Spring 1980): 31–38.

Saghafi, Kas. "The Death Penalty, in Other Words, Philosophy." *Southern Journal of Philosophy 50*, Spindel Supplement (2012): 136–142.

Sarat, Austin. *Gruesome Spectacles: Botched Executions and America's Death Penalty*. Stanford, Calif.: Stanford Law Books, 2014.

———, ed. *The Killing State: Capital Punishment in Law, Politics, and Culture*. Oxford: Oxford University Press, 2001.

Schabas, William. *The Abolition of the Death Penalty in International Law*. Cambridge: Cambridge University Press, 1993, 1997.

Schlosser, Eric. "The Prison-Industrial Complex." *Atlantic Monthly*,

December 1998. http://www.theatlantic.com/magazine/archive/1998/
12/the-prison-industrial-complex/304669/.

Schmeiser, Susan R. "Waiving from Death Row." In *Who Deserves to Die?:
Constructing the Executable Subject*, ed. Austin Sarat and Karl Shoemaker. Amherst: University of Massachusetts Press, 2011.

Schofer, Peter. "*Une mort héroïque*: Baudelaire's Social Theater of Cruelty." *French Literature Series 15* (1988): 50–57.

Sentein, François. *L'assassin et son bourreau: Jean Genet et Maurice
Pilorge*. Arles: Actes Sud, 1999.

Smith, Amy. "Not 'Waiving' but Drowning: The Anatomy of Death Row
Syndrome and Volunteering for Execution." *Public Interest Law Journal* 17 (2008): 237–254.

UN News Centre. "Still Far Too Much Secrecy Surrounding Use of Death
Penalty, Says Senior UN Human Rights Official." November 21, 2017.
http://www.un.org/apps/news/story.asp?NewsID=58138#
.WiWEj0tryis.

Walsh, Richard. "Narrative Inscription, History, and the Reader in Robert
Coover's *The Public Burning*." *Studies in the Novel* 25, no. 3 (Fall
1993): 332–346.

Wilbur, Robert. "The True Crime of the Rosenberg Execution." *Truthout*,
June 19, 2011. http://www.truth-out.org/news/item/1537:the-true
-crime-of-the-rosenberg-execution.

Wills, David. "Drone Penalty." *SubStance* 43, no. 2 (2014): 174–192.

Wilson, Andrew. "American Minimalism: The American Vernacular in Norman Mailer's *The Executioner's Song*." *European Journal of American
Studies* 4, no. 1 (Spring 2009): 2–14.

Wing, Nathaniel. "Poets, Mimes, and Counterfeit Coins: On Power and
Discourse in Baudelaire's Prose Poetry." *Paragraph* 13, no. 1 (March
1990): 1–18.

Wright, Richard. *Native Son*. New York: Perennial Classics, 1989.

INDEX

 INVENTING WRITING THEORY
Jacques Lezra and Paul North, series editors

Werner Hamacher, *Minima Philologica*. Translated by Catharine Diehl and
Jason Groves

Michal Ben-Naftali, *Chronicle of Separation: On Deconstruction's Disillusioned
Love*. Translated by Mirjam Hadar. Foreword by Avital Ronell

Daniel Hoffman-Schwartz, Barbara Natalie Nagel, and Lauren Shizuko Stone,
eds., *Flirtations: Rhetoric and Aesthetics This Side of Seduction*

Jean-Luc Nancy, *Intoxication*. Translated by Philip Armstrong

Márton Dornbach, *Receptive Spirit: German Idealism and the Dynamics of
Cultural Transmission*

Sean Alexander Gurd, *Dissonance: Auditory Aesthetics in Ancient Greece*

Anthony Curtis Adler, *Celebricities: Media Culture and the Phenomenology
of Gadget Commodity Life*

Nathan Brown, *The Limits of Fabrication: Materials Science, Materialist
Poetics*

Jay Bernstein, Adi Ophir, and Ann Laura Stoler, eds., *Political Concepts:
A Critical Lexicon*

Peggy Kamuf, *Literature and the Remains of the Death Penalty*